SLA | GUIDELINES
plus

Cool, Calm and Collected

Managing Behaviour in the Secondary School Library

Claire Larson
and Geoff Dubber

Series Editor: Geoff Dubber

Acknowledgements

Many thanks to that multitude of young people who we have had the privilege to teach and work with in secondary school libraries.

Our thanks also go to all the school librarians whose real-life comments and opinions we have quoted liberally throughout this book and to Barbara Band, Ann Cowdrey, Frances Sinclair and Laura Taylor for their case studies.

We would also like to thank Sally Duncan and Liz Smith for their very helpful comments on the text of this Guideline and as ever our very grateful thanks go to Richard Leveridge and Jane Cooper for their excellent work as part of the Publications Team – without their expertise, dedication and team work there would be no publications.

Published by

School Library Association
Unit 2, Lotmead Business Village,
Wanborough, Swindon SN4 0UY

Tel: +44 (0)1793 791787 Fax: +44 (0)1793 791786
E-mail: info@sla.org.uk
Web: www.sla.org.uk

Registered Charity No: 313660
Charity Registered in Scotland No: SC039453

Cover photographs by Martin Salter
Printed by Information Press, Eynsham, Oxford

Contents

"

Act the way you'd like to be
and soon you'll be the way you act.

— George W. Crane

My child, from your youth choose discipline,
and when you have grey hair you will still find wisdom.

— Ecclesiasticus 6.18, noticed on a 17th-century
tomb in Ely Cathedral by one of the authors

[Some] adults find it extraordinarily
difficult to give children the respect they deserve.

— David Gribble

"

Please note:

For the purposes of this publication the terms school library and
LRC – learning/library resource centre – are interchangeable.

Many things tax the wit and wisdom of school librarians, none more so than the behaviour of their users – both students and adults. Of all the issues that fill the school librarian discussion forums and listservs, behaviour is always a hot topic. Managing user behaviour and creating a supportive and relaxed learning environment are fundamental aims for everyone who runs a school Library Resources Centre. Responding to the varied needs of hundreds of people, both staff and students, can be rewarding, especially when the LRC is viewed as a valued part of the school and is central to learning. It's useful to remember that you are usually the only person in the entire school who serves the learning and teaching needs of everyone. However, if things go wrong and they do everywhere sometimes, if the cool and calm atmosphere of the LRC becomes fraught, the resulting tensions, confrontations and staff stress can seriously undermine students' experience of learning and the self-confidence of LRC staff.

These are a range of upsetting happenings and scenarios:

I am sending this message from home as I'm not likely to be in school next week. I had a dreadful week: first a bad session with a Y9 student shouting the odds at me, then I had a Y12 student who persisted in playing computer games having been warned 3 times...

At lunchtime I had a gang of Y10 boys in the library, many of whom have only just been allowed in after a ban for bad behaviour. One boy thinks it's acceptable to eat his lunch in the library leaving food wrappers and food remains everywhere.

Just had a ghastly lesson with a Y8 class. The teacher was a supply teacher who came in looked at me saying 'what are we doing' (as if it's my job to know – what about the English teacher who left the class?)

We have a spate of girls coming into the library specifically to push all the fiction books to the back of the shelf.

I am really upset by an incident this afternoon – a part-time student started chatting on her mobile phone and then told me to shut up when I asked her to turn it off and ran into the toilets to carry on chatting.

I think that we are pretty typical here in that lunchtimes are an absolute nightmare, especially in the Autumn and Spring Terms. I am on my own with upwards of 70 students in the library and adjacent computer room. Very often it resembles a tumble dryer!

I am considering buying tables with attached chairs for my library as the students keep on moving the chairs around, ending up with big groups around one table.

I have just had a horrendous session with my line manager, who seems to believe that the spate of bad behaviour is entirely due to my negativity and the fact that I shout at the boys too much.

I have just had an arrogant senior colleague stalk into the library, demand silence from everyone as that's what we should have in the school library, glare at me and walk out again. Talk about rudeness!

Does anyone else get frustrated by the TAs allowing pupils to access games as a reward when the pupils have finished their work? We have a blanket ban on games and this is clearly stated on a notice on each PC, but the TAs accompanying small groups to the library don't ever seem to think that it applies to them! I've had a couple of verbal tussles with them...

The ethos of most schools and school libraries is excellent, but the issue of behaviour in and out of school, with knife crime and bullying in particular has been on many agendas over several years. We had for instance Tony Blair's Respect Agenda in early 2006 that caught the attention of the media. Or a headline in the *TES* 'Knife carrying youths face automatic prosecution as street violence spirals'.[1] Of course we all have an opinion, often shaped by political spin and hair raising stories in the media. There is no doubt that the behaviour of children in our schools and its impact on their achievement and their developing perception of libraries is of prime concern to all of us.

Behaviour surveys

Behaviour in schools has been a focus for governments across the United Kingdom and in the Republic of Ireland in recent years. Some interesting surveys have been carried out, work done and reports written. We list a selection of these in the 'Reports' section of Appendix 8. They include:

- *Behaviour in Wales. Good Practice in Managing Challenging Behaviour.* (Estyn had produced some useful Behaviour Management Training two years earlier.)

- *School Matters: a Report by the Task Force on Student Behaviour in Second Level Schools*, 2006, was produced in the Republic of Ireland.

- In Scotland, *Case Studies of Good Practice in Improving the Climate for Learning* October, 2006, mentions behaviour 167 times in 35 pages.

- *Behaviour in Scottish Schools* – some research from the NFER for the Scottish Executive 2005/2006 is well worth a read.

- Scotland also has some excellent website material: *Behaviour4Learning* and *Better Behaviour in Scotland*.

- In England, OFSTED produced an excellent report in 2005 – *Managing Challenging Behaviour* – and also another as a follow up in November 2006 – *Improving Behaviour: Lessons Learned From HMI Monitoring of Secondary Schools Where Behaviour Had Been Judged Unsatisfactory.* The DCSF has also made sure that Behaviour and Attendance is a key part of its work to raise attainment across Key Stage 3 as a part of its

[1] *Time Educational Supplement 5 June 2008, p.5*

Secondary National Strategy. There are messages, toolkits, training materials and case studies all with a behaviour and attendance theme to them. More recently the launch of 'Secondary SEAL' – Social and Emotional Aspects for Learning – clearly involves behaviour and social interaction.

More recently new guidelines have been issued to schools concerning behaviour and discipline. School governors now have a statutory responsibility for determining their school's ethos with regard to disciplinary matters. This involves writing and generally reviewing a statement based on the school's values of what the DCSF call 'general principles of how pupils should behave and relate to one another and to others'... the statement must comply with equalities legislation and have regard for the well being of pupils... There's also a legal requirement... to consult with the Head Teacher, teachers, parents and pupils...[2] Schools now have a legal right to discipline children, including for poor behaviour beyond school and to confiscate property.[3]

Perhaps the behaviour report that received the most media coverage was *Learning Behaviour*, the report of the Practitioners' Group on School Behaviour and Discipline.[4] Chaired by Sir Alan Steer, Head Teacher of Seven Kings High School in Essex, this report outlined a whole range of positive strategies – 'one major section of our report offers advice to our fellow practitioners on the kind of practical approaches which can work in schools.'[5]

None of the resources listed above overtly mentions the school library, but all apply to its policies and daily strategies and operation. With this in mind, and because the library is an integral part of the working of all effective schools, we have revised and extended this Guideline adopting some of the practical and common sense principles outlined in that report and related here to the LRC, namely that:

- The environment in which we study, learn, relax and work influences our behaviour.

- Clear rewards and sanctions, which are in line with school policy, and which are applied fairly and consistently, help to promote good behaviour in the LRC.

---

[2] *On Best Behaviour* p. 12 Report. Association of Teachers and Lecturers. Sept. 2007
[3] http://www.teachernet.gov.uk/wholeschool/behaviour/ schooldisciplinepupilbehaviourpolicies/
See also http://www.atl.org.uk/factsheets
[4] Steer, 2005
[5] Extract from Sir Alan Steer's letter submitting the report to the government.

- Good behaviour is learned. We all have a responsibility to teach it and model it.

- Specific strategies can be adopted in various circumstances such as managing student behaviour during a lesson in the LRC, during free time in the LRC and when individuals or small groups use the LRC.

- The LRC staff should be involved in all aspects of training and coaching regarding behaviour management.

This Guideline takes each principle and shows how it can be applied straightforwardly and successfully in a busy LRC. It suggests a range of strategies for promoting good behaviour and effective use of the LRC and also places great emphasis on the importance of the LRC staff's status in school, their self esteem and professional development. These factors are intricately linked to the ethos of the LRC, its atmosphere and the resultant behaviour.

Good behaviour is not something that just happens. A skilled teacher may hold a large group of pupils in the palm of her hand, so that all are focused, motivated and learning effectively. Managing their behaviour is an important element of this and something which is covered during teacher training and professional development. For LRC staff the learning curve can be far steeper. They usually have very little induction and then learn on the job, often receiving little guidance or advice, and their first experience of managing students may be during a wet lunchtime when the library is overflowing with noisy, excitable teenagers.

If you really want to develop your behaviour management skills with young people then remember the 3 Ls!

LOOK, LISTEN and LEARN from those colleagues in school who you feel are good with people, and students in particular. Watch their body language and timing, listen to their tone and their words. If you're impressed with them, then tell them so. Ask to sit in on/join them for one of their lessons and see them in action in the classroom. We all like praise and not only will you learn by observation but you're likely to have made a useful ally to support you next time you have a behaviour issue.

LRC staff are not teachers in the sense that they are not directly responsible for a particular subject, nor for the continuous and progressive learning of groups of children. However, they have direct and daily contact with students across the school and are uniquely involved in their learning. Developments in ICT and the demand that students work independently to find and handle information gives LRC staff a significant role in supporting the curriculum. It is essential to create a purposeful learning environment which promotes the appropriate behaviour.

A hint before you start to apply the following strategies and ideas to your LRC – many factors affect the behaviour of young people in the LRC – some of them you can certainly influence, others you cannot. Look through the following list and decide which ones you can personally influence.

- You as a person, your style, status and situation
- Your perceptions of yourself and your job and the relating body language
- School ethos and morale
- Students, their personal attitudes and situations
- Teaching and learning styles used and encouraged across the whole school
- The school environment
- The LRC environment
- LRC resources
- The time of day/season of the year
- Last night's football results
- Last night's domestic/social happenings at home and within the community
- A school inspection
- Food and drug intake of the pupils

When you study the list it quickly becomes apparent that library staff cannot affect very many of these factors. Our advice from the start is to work hard on the ones that you can change and ignore those beyond your control. Focus your effort where it can really make a difference rather than worry about other factors.

Which face suits you at work?

Which will promote better behaviour?

Section One: The Environment

The environment in which we study, learn, relax and work influences our behaviour.

For our purpose **The Environment** encompasses the physical location of the LRC and less tangible aspects such as:

- School ethos
- The LRC staff – their perceived status and working conditions, especially in the current climate of Workforce Reform
- Staff perceptions of the LRC
- Student perceptions of the LRC
- Parents' perceptions of the LRC
- The physical environment.

Student behaviour is influenced by many factors…

> *'They're always more unpredictable when it's a windy day…'*

> *'Christmas? The last few days of term are damage limitation and crisis management!'*

> *'The mock GCSEs have started and I've never seen year 11 look so stressed…'*

Some of these factors are associated with the experience, self confidence and perceptions of LRC staff, some with whole school attitudes and others specifically with the LRC and its environment. Some we can control, others – the weather, the time of year or a friendship crisis we cannot, and of course, it's vital to remember that we all, students and staff, have an off day sometimes.

So how does the environment play such an important part in promoting good behaviour?

School Ethos

You can't always see it, but you know it's there. It's that intangible atmosphere and spirit that characterises the whole school. To work effectively it must be positive, supportive and all embracing. It can be the difference between a ripped and ancient classroom display and the Deputy Head talking football with Year 10 in the corridor at break time. It can be the difference between a hive of industry in the LRC during breakfast club at 8.15am and a stack of tired paperbacks circa 1989 gracing the library shelves.

The school is a community and all staff play an important part in developing and promoting a caring ethos that supports learning and positive behaviour. This caring ethos is a two way street and staff, in turn should receive support, encouragement and a feeling of worth while undertaking their job.

Workforce Reform

There have been many changes to the school workforce in recent years, resulting in an increase in the number of support staff working directly with students. A few years ago LRC staff and teaching assistants were the only ones fulfilling this role. Today a school is likely to have a multitude of support staff:

- Learning Managers/Cover supervisors – who cover lessons for absent teachers
- Year Managers – who take on the pastoral role as head of year
- Learning Mentors – who work with targeted youngsters to improve their learning
- School Counsellors
- Teaching Assistants
- Higher Level Teaching Assistants
- Learning Support Staff
- LRC staff.

This has had the advantage of raising the profile of support staff in schools.

'There was a time when we used to feel uncomfortable if we sat in the staff room, now we attend staff briefing there every morning.'

'Thankfully the days when we were referred to as "Non Teachers" and "Ancillary Staff" have long gone.'

'I am treated as a head of department and have to submit my Annual Development Plan to justify my budget. It's hard work, but I feel valued.'

'I recently passed my GNVQ level four. The school really supported me while I was doing it and I've just been promoted.'

LRC Staff Status

How you feel about your position within the work place affects how you do your job. The status and self confidence of LRC staff is extremely important. Equal status with teaching colleagues and the full confidence of senior management are essential to all aspects of the job, including managing behaviour.

This whole issue of behaviour is tied up with how the library is regarded in the school as a whole, and **you will get nowhere without support and backing from senior teaching staff.**

Problems are more likely to arise where LRC staff feel isolated and undervalued. Even though workforce reform has increased support staff numbers, the LRC staff may still feel isolated as unlike other support staff such as teaching assistants and learning managers they are less likely to be part of a team, or linked to a specific department. They may feel they are working alone and must therefore cope with problems on their own.

It is vital to feel a part of the school community and there are strategies that can be adopted to make this happen:

- Make sure you have a clear job description and opportunities for professional development.

- Have a clear line management structure and regular meetings with your line manager so that successes and challenge, including those that concern behaviour can be discussed.

- Make a point of meeting regularly with teaching colleagues both formally and informally.

  'I always attend Head of Department meetings to make sure I'm up to date with what's going on and can plan LRC usage accordingly.'

  'I work so closely with the Humanities faculty that I was invited to their Christmas do.'

- Keep up to date with school developments and current issues.

- Make sure information about the LRC is highlighted in staff and school handbooks and on the school website.

- Join and perhaps lead appropriate staff INSET sessions.

- Be part of the school inspection process.

- Network through your SLS and SLA branch with neighbouring colleagues in other schools and other types of library.

- Maintain your professional development. Read about library issues – we recommend that you read all the relevant SLA publications and attend training courses.

Check out your present status and working conditions with Appendix 1. As a rule of thumb, there is a direct correlation between the number of ticks and the level of behaviour problems.

Working conditions

LRC staff frequently work alone and arrangements concerning working routines can be haphazard. It is not unusual for workloads to increase suddenly so that services may be developed. Managing pupils is challenging enough, but will be almost impossible if LRC staff are working long hours with insufficient help and support and eating a snatched ten minute lunch while preparing resources for the next lesson.

A 'well being' programme run by the Teacher Support Network[6] proved clearly that caring for staff helped improve behaviour across a school. In a survey associated with this programme, 85% of Norfolk head teachers believed that pupil behaviour had improved because of the TLC given to the teaching staff.[7] The same will clearly apply to library staff. Better morale, attainment and staff retention was also noticeable. If you're not being offered much TLC by your line manager, then do your best to look after yourself.

- Allow yourself some time away from the LRC.

  'I close the LRC twice a week at break time so I can go in the staff room. The students sometimes complain, but I need the opportunity to catch up with people. Some of our best LRC projects have been planned over a cup of coffee...'

- Do the maths with your student numbers! Establish the numbers you can realistically manage and be prepared to turn students away once the LRC is full.

  'I worked so hard to make the LRC exciting and inviting that I ended up with queues at the door at lunch time and I just couldn't cope with the sheer numbers. I talked to my line manager and we decided to divide the lunch time into two sessions – one session for the lower school and one for the upper school. It's working well and I don't feel quite so frazzled!'

- Make sure you feel comfortable with the number and activities of those using ICT in the library.

  'The students are only allowed on the internet for research purposes, but it's an uphill struggle keeping them off games and ringtone sites. The Head of ICT is really supportive and we block persistent offenders from the ICT equipment for up to a week. They soon get the message.'

- Ensure that working conditions are agreed in writing with your line manager. Discuss any changes or service developments in terms not only of the benefit for students and the school, but also of how they will be managed by you. Be conscious of Health and Safety issues – for the students and for yourself.

---

[6] *TES* 14 February 2003
[7] For information about The Well –Being Programme see
    http://www.worklifesupport.com/index.cfm?a=201

LRC Staff — on top of the world or going under?

Library staff themselves have the biggest impact on managing behaviour in the LRC. A sense of humour is essential when working with staff and students. Adults who are usually rather glum and feel under siege and under stress, tend to see young people as hostile and those feelings clearly show in body language, general demeanour and the way that we talk with others. An outgoing, cheerful personality will help things to run smoothly.

Which face best suits you at work and why?

It's pretty obvious which one the staff and students are going to warm to and which one is likely to influence positive and responsive behaviour! Some people have taken to displaying these simple images on their office wall to remember themselves of the importance of a public face.

Sometimes opting for 'top of the world' rather than 'going under' entails a bit of acting. Every day, when meeting and working with students we put on a performance. We may feel disillusioned or irritable, but it's vital to appear cheerful, confident and in control. Sometimes this will come easily, at other times we will deserve an Oscar. It will be most helpful during a busy lunchtime when we are the only adult in charge of thirty, forty or even more youngsters. They need to know that we are in charge, and to get that message across try to remember the 4 Cs.

 CALM

 CHEERFUL

 CONFIDENT

 IN CONTROL

Staff Perceptions of the LRC

Staff perceptions vary and we have probably all come across most of the following:

The LRC is…

- The perfect place to encourage students to think for themselves and do homework which specifically requires them to use the LRC.
- Somewhere peaceful to catch up with my marking.

- The ideal venue to encourage children to read.
- Somewhere for year 7 to sit when they've forgotten their PE kit.
- The best place to help pupils develop their information handling skills.
- A place where three people can sit the history exam they missed.
- The venue for a School Council meeting.
- Somewhere for students to surf the Net or type up coursework.
- The best place for meetings between mentors and students.
- Somewhere to send disruptive Year 10 pupils to get them out of the way.

The LRC may well be used for all these purposes and more, but clearly some are more acceptable than others. It will be difficult to promote a purposeful, learning environment if the library is used variously as sin-bin, waiting room and examination room. Our advice is to be assertive. You have control of the space so make sure it's used for purposes that you find worthwhile. LRC as dumping ground and detention space are not acceptable (and never were actually!)

Staff perception of the LRC and its staff is extremely important. Teachers' opinions are easily transmitted to pupils. If teachers and support staff value the LRC this is more likely to be reflected in their students' enthusiasm and positive behaviour. Section 2 looks at ways to promote 'good' use of the LRC by creating and displaying an LRC Policy and code of conduct.

Have a look at Appendix 2 Perceptions – it might prove helpful to your thinking.

Student Perceptions of the LRC

These will vary among the students just as much as they do among staff and the LRC may be viewed as…

- Somewhere to do homework, revise for the imminent French test and watch the video we missed in English.
- A place to meet up during a wet lunch-time.
- Somewhere to surf the Net.
- Where all the geeks hang out, there's nothing for me there.
- The best place to find the latest Darren Shan or Robert Muchamore.
- A bolt hole, the only place I feel safe at break time.
- Somewhere to relax and read the *Guinness Book of Records* or the latest fashion magazines.
- Somewhere I can be myself and explore my interests

One of the most successful ways to encourage effective use of the LRC and maintain positive behaviour is to ensure that students know what is expected of them. The induction programme is an excellent place to start and is a way of introducing students to what's on offer and equally importantly an opportunity to outline your expectations of them when they use the LRC.

Different schools and LRCs have different expectations, pet hates, irritations and difficulties.

> 'Our school insists that mobile phones are switched off and out of sight. If I catch someone playing with their phone in the library, I confiscate it and pass it to their head of year.'

> 'During induction I teach year 7 the mnemonic CBC meaning coats off, bags on the floor and sit on a chair. This is what I expect of them when they come into the LRC at lunchtime as well as during lessons. and I'm quite happy to remind them until they remember automatically.'

Developing an LRC policy and code of conduct is another way of shaping student perceptions and therefore behaviour: this is dealt with fully in the next section.

Parents' Perceptions of the LRC

If the parents have a very positive perception of the LRC and all that it does to support learning and reading across the school, this can have a very positive effect on students' behaviour. To make these links with parents the library should feature clearly in the school prospectus, other school documentation and in school publicity and events. If library staff are seen and can be available for discussion – perhaps even to put on a reading presentation or a family quiz on parents evening – this is all to the good.

The Physical Environment

> 'All schools should recognise that good behaviour and learning are improved when pupils and staff enjoy an attractive, clean environment.'
> — Steer Report.[8]

We can all sense atmosphere quite quickly. Remember what it felt like in the last hotel or B & B that you used – the sights, the smells and the welcome?

The LRC environment, its furniture, fittings and general ambiance transmit a powerful message and one of the most exciting things that LRC staff can do is to shape the library environment and atmosphere and make it inclusive.

We would all like to be in charge of a purpose built, spacious, airy, beautifully decorated, fantastically resourced and furnished LRC but many of us are more likely to be in a space originally designed for something else completely…

---

[8] Steer, 2005

'My library is the old school hall, a fantastic size, but with such a high ceiling the slightest noise really echoes.'

'The LRC is housed in what used to be two classrooms. The floors are on slightly different levels so there are certain areas where it's impossible to have shelving.'

'We've been promised a brand new school in 2012 complete with state of the art LRC, but until then my library can seat a maximum of thirty students.'

You may not be running the ideal LRC (although with the BSF programme[9] many more library staff are now working in better purpose built LRCs) but there is still a lot that can be done to ensure that it is welcoming and nurtures the appropriate behaviour:

Layout

Where possible the position of shelving and furniture should help to create an uncluttered environment with clear lines of vision and no hidden areas which are an invitation for misbehaviour.

'When I first started here we had enormous conference tables that could seat sixteen. The students hated them because they couldn't concentrate with all the distractions. It took me eighteen months and a lot of canvassing, but we now have small tables that can be grouped when necessary and the students seem far more relaxed now they can work individually or in smaller groups.'

'I make all the shelf signs myself. The student librarians get involved too, downloading suitable pictures to go with each Dewey section. The end result looks professional and helps give the right impression – that the LRC is well organised, smart and user friendly.'

Seating

Many LRCs offer comfortable seating areas and even cushions, beanbags and sofas to encourage students to relax and read. The downside is that these areas are also popular with students who want to congregate for a chat. The Steer report recommends that 'social areas in the school are identified and seating provided to encourage pupils to interact.'[10] Of course that would happen in an ideal world, but inevitably lack of social spaces becomes a real problem, especially during an icy winter break time when the LRC suddenly becomes a very desirable place to be!

If comfortable seating arrangements do cause problems consider placing them where supervision is easier, perhaps near the LRC desk. Display books

---

[9] Building Schools for the Future, a building programme affecting state secondary schools across England.
http://www.teachernet.gov.uk/management/resourcesfinanceandbuilding/bsf/
[10] Steer, 2005.

and magazines nearby to reinforce the message that the seating is for quiet reading. If the problem persists consider putting the chairs and cushions into storage for a while and reintroduce them gradually as the atmosphere improves.

'We offer beanbags as part of our loyalty scheme. Regular (sensible!) students can book them in advance at lunch time and I have very few problems, but I would recommend spending a bit more money and getting cushions with removable covers that will go through the washing machine!'

Displays

LRC staff have a deservedly high reputation as would-be *Blue Peter* presenters – experts on creating eye-catching, professional displays with little money and bags of creative talent. Not only do these help to make the LRC relevant and interesting, but by displaying examples of work, pupils gain an even greater sense of ownership. Displays can also be used to give students ideas for work on specific projects, ask questions of them, develop their thinking further and also provide information to help with location of resources, Dewey numbers, keywords, etc.

'For World Book Day, I ran a competition to design book covers and we laminated and displayed the winning entries. It generated a lot of interest and pupils were delighted to see their work and that of their friends on show.'

'I always have a "puzzle of the day" on display, usually a brainteaser and the first one to solve it gets a merit.'

'At the beginning of the Autumn term I make sure my word wall is up to date with library vocabulary – and I always refer to it during induction sessions.'

Tidiness

How clean is your LRC?

Chipping chewing gum off the carpet and dusting computer keyboards is rarely part of the LRC job description, but how the LRC looks can have a huge impact on student attitude and therefore behaviour. Behaviour is always likely to be more positive and responsive if the shelves are tidy, furniture is not constantly being shifted, displays are in good condition and up to date and the counter and entrance/exit areas are uncluttered and welcoming.

'I always keep cleaning materials to hand and clean up any graffiti on tables immediately. As a result the library is a completely graffiti free zone.'

'My student librarians are responsible for keeping the magazine rack neat and tidy and they take the job very seriously.'

'My student librarians have their own noticeboard in the office where they can leave messages for each other and I can keep them up to date with anything they need to know.'

Resources

It may seem strange to mention resources in a guideline about behaviour, but they do have an important bearing on the attitude of LRC customers. They need to be varied and current and must also reflect the needs and interests of the entire school population.

'When I first started working here the Head boasted proudly that there were twenty thousand books in the library. That may have been true but some of them hadn't been taken off the shelf for over ten years! To start with the students were really dismissive of the library and their behaviour reflected that. The library was just a place where you could mess around. Within two years I had removed about six thousand books and concentrated on buying lots of popular fiction and plenty of study guides to attract my customers. Attitudes have changed and now the library is a highly regarded hub of the school.'

Resources also need to be clearly accessible. User behaviour will be improved if the students confidently handle the classification scheme, the loan system and ICT based materials and understand how to make use of your bay and shelf guides. Students who are more independent will use the resources with increased ease and behaviour will generally improve.

Use of ICT

In many libraries ICT location and more importantly use, is problematic. As we all know to the frustration of many of our colleagues, many students use it as the first port of call for an enquiry and it is not unknown for teachers to send students to the LRC simply for word processing tasks. Students commonly attempt to circumvent agreed user policies and many librarians spend a good deal of time and effort managing this sort of behaviour.

Constant vigilance, clear display of agreed policies and working with individuals on a one to one basis form the usual behaviour policies but use of monitoring software can also be really helpful. Library staff can view web pages currently being accessed by students, any previously used and other programs being used. Reminder messages can be sent to the student, their screen can be blanked or access denied completely.

As a strategy to help to improve behaviour in the LRC and maximise librarian supervision of ICT, this software has much to recommend it. See Appendix 4 for some examples of student monitoring software.

Section Two: Rewards and Sanctions

Clear rewards and sanctions, which are in line with school policy, and which are applied fairly and consistently, help to promote good behaviour in the Library Resources Centre.

Having strategies for coping with bad behaviour and encouraging good behaviour is essential. Any school or person who leaves this to chance is inviting problems.

'I have a cunning plan...'
Having a plan means that you have already considered the negative things that pupils may do and that you have thought about the kinds of responses available to you. This section looks at the overall strategies the LRC might adopt to manage problems with behaviour. The next section looks in detail at ways you as an individual might manage specific incidents of problem behaviour in the LRC.

Most plans will, even should, begin with a working knowledge of the school behaviour policy and how this can be put into action to help YOU!

Behaviour Policies

All schools have a behaviour policy. Indeed Alan Steer's report outlined the possibility of creating a National Behaviour Charter setting out the responsibilities of schools, pupils and parents in promoting good behaviour. (This has yet to happen). Specific rules or sanctions would be left to the discretion of individual schools; it is however, interesting that such a charter has been considered. Clearly behaviour and the effect on learning are of national significance.

Any school policy regarding behaviour should be clear, well communicated to both staff and students and, most importantly, consistently put into practice. Obviously this is the responsibility of the school's senior managers, and is hopefully well covered during staff induction and INSET sessions. However, LRC staff have their own responsibilities. The LRC as a central part of the school, used potentially by all pupils, needs to operate in line with any behaviour policy.

LRC staff should be familiar with it and USE it! Your job will be more straightforward if students know that the same codes of behaviour apply in the LRC as elsewhere in the school. Make sure that you:

- Familiarise yourself with the school behaviour policy and the systems for putting it into action.

- Discuss with teaching colleagues how they use the policy in practice.

- Follow any set procedures for reporting and following up behaviour problems.

This approach has two benefits. Firstly, pupils realise that the same is expected of them in the LRC as elsewhere in the school. Secondly, teaching colleagues will appreciate that you are following accepted and agreed procedures. For example, if a problem with behaviour is always reported to the form tutor in the first instance it would be wrong for LRC staff to take a problem straight to the head of year as this undermines collective attempts to operate sanctions and promote good behaviour throughout the school. You may even find certain forms have to be filled in and passed on to appropriate people and it's only fair that LRC staff should follow the correct procedure.

> 'My induction didn't cover what to do when students misbehave. I was given a copy of the policy but no one went through it with me. Then in my first week two students had a fight in the library and I had to call for help. After that I asked the deputy head to go through the policy with me so I could be clear about handling everyday incidents and emergencies. She then helped me to formulate the code of conduct which is specific to the library but in line with the behaviour policy. It's worked a treat and everyone knows what's expected and what will happen if the code isn't adhered to.'

If you find the policies and procedures fail in practice, then don't just ignore them but point out to senior management, in a positive manner, those aspects that appear to you to be failing.

If you feel particularly harassed by one individual or group who seem to persist in upsetting you, then view it as bullying and use that word when discussing the situation with your line manager. Schools usually take a strong line with bullying so to use the word will usually help your case and action is more likely to be taken for resolution.

It is easy to convince yourself, especially if you feel stressed and perhaps a little inadequate, that students are only playing up in the library. this is unlikely. Chat with other staff and you will almost certainly find that patterns of poor behaviour are repeated elsewhere too. Sharing concerns and strategies will usually provide you with a good deal of support.

You cannot change the climate on your own

As the proverb says, 'It takes a whole village to educate a child'.

There is undoubtedly a link between pupils' behaviour around the school and their behaviour in the library. We wrote earlier that school ethos embraces the attitude and spirit that characterises the whole school. If that ethos is positive and nurturing a behaviour policy will be in place that everyone knows and 95% of people will adhere to. Praise for good behaviour will far outstrip the need for sanctions and everyone will know the rules and most will play by them. From time to time problems with behaviour will arise and you will feel you have the tools to deal with them effectively. Alternatively if you work in a school where behaviour is poor generally you may be up against far worse problems with behaviour in the LRC. You will be able to adopt short term solutions, but in the long term this is a problem too great to be handled alone. On your own you cannot change the school ethos, and behaviour management will need to be addressed as a whole school issue. If you feel that behaviour issues are serious, depressing and stressful on a daily basis we suggest that you change schools. Your own physical and mental health and well being is of prime importance.

The Code of Conduct

Many schools have clear behaviour targets on display in corridors and class rooms. These may cover issues such as walking on the left, no chewing, putting your hand up before speaking or taking care of equipment and possessions. You may feel that the LRC requires its own clear and concise policy outlining expectations of behaviour.

The Steer Report reminds us that any policy should be clear, well communicated and most importantly put into practice! There is little point in a long list of rules and regulations, stuck up on a wall somewhere and never referred to again. If you do decide to come up with your own LRC code of conduct bear in mind the following:

Keep it simple.

Stick to a few well-chosen and positive phrases to remind pupils what is expected of them.

Publicise it.

You could include the code of conduct on the LRC membership card if you have them. Display it by the LRC desk or on the notice board and ensure it is part of the LRC induction programme.

Use it.

If a pupil misbehaves, point out which part of the code they are not keeping to. Congratulate pupils for following it.

'I kept my code of conduct to the initials LRC emphasising the importance of Learning, Responsibility and Consideration.'

'I used to have problems with students wandering around the library aimlessly and getting themselves into mischief. I rewrote the code of conduct and one of my rules is that all students using the library must be actively engaged, whether it's doing homework, reading or playing draughts. I drew attention to this regularly and the problem has just about disappeared.'

'I have the code of conduct on display and I find it effective to bring the misbehaving student to the notice board to point out exactly which part of the code they are breaking.'

I've got my code of conduct. What next?

You know the school policy on behaviour and you feel confident in putting it into practice. You have a code of conduct which is on display, taught and referred to regularly. However, whatever tools are in place, problems with behaviour will arise and need to be dealt with.

Rewards and Sanctions

The Steer report reminds us that there should be a balance between rewards and sanctions. Praise is vital to motivate and encourage students, but they also need to be aware that sanctions are in place should they choose to misbehave.

As a rule rewards should outstrip sanctions.

Why reward?
The key here is to 'catch them being good'. It is far easier and more pleasurable to reward good behaviour than it is to punish bad. If you are rewarding good behaviour then all parties are in a 'win/win' situation. You're pleased and proud because the student has done well. They are pleased because their good behaviour has been noticed and praised. Result, both parties are motivated to continue the cycle of good behaviour, praise and reward.

If you are constantly having to draw attention to bad behaviour, tell students off and punish them you are far more likely to find yourself in a negative 'lose/lose' situation. You become disillusioned and fed up with the constant bad behaviour and students are tired of being told off and are more likely to react with further bouts of bad behaviour. Result both parties are de-motivated and a negative cycle of misbehaving, punishment and more misbehaviour is likely to arise.

The solution is to praise consistently and regularly. This is especially powerful for certain students who have settled into a cycle of misbehaving. 'If you tell a pupil often enough that he is a disruptive influence he will surrender to the title and become it even more.'[11]

When giving praise, aim to make it:

■ Personal
> *'That's really impressive Mathew – I couldn't do as well. Mr Smith is bound to be very impressed.'*

■ Regular
Try to talk to all your frequent users on a regular basis – with positive comment. They will look forward to talking with you.
> *'Hey – this is the second time this week I've praised you – you must be doing well.'*

Remember that frequent negative comments or grumbles appeal to nobody.

---

[11] Dunn, 2005

Appropriate
Don't get too carried away, or it may seem insincere. However, it is really important to show your enthusiasm and genuine warmth for individuals and groups. It will raise their self-esteem no end and they will think so much more about the LRC and its role.

Informed
If you know the person or group the praise becomes more personal and meaningful.

> 'When I think back to your behaviour last year – you are really grown up and sensible now, thanks for helping out with that project.'

Spontaneous
Make sure your enthusiasm and interest in the person or groups comes through – spontaneity always looks very genuine.

Effective
Praise should be regular but not too frequent, sincere but not too 'over the top' and not too loud or public as to cause embarrassment.

What reward?

We all enjoy receiving a reward – a word of praise as positive feedback or something more tangible. Most schools have a reward system, perhaps involving house points, merits or privilege passes and you may wish to adopt that. It's important to remember though that some schools only like to give merits for learning achievement. The LRC staff are in the enviable position of being able to reward privately and individually for just about anything. A word of praise is often appropriate (and better than anything more tangible). It is important to remember that in the normal way you **cannot over praise** (given the provisos of the previous paragraph). Behaviour experts and child psychologists tell us that **the ratio of praise to correction should be at least 6 to 1.** In other words you should praise a pupil six times for every correction that you give them. We cannot emphasise this enough; praise whenever possible, even if it is for something ordinary and basic that you would expect.

The praise reward is an ideal opportunity to model behaviour that you like and wish to see continue, for example:

> 'Well done year 7, you came into the LRC really sensibly today.'

> 'Thank you for picking that book up off the floor Steven.'

> 'I think it's great that you are teaching Farzana how to play chess. Well done.'

> 'Your book is back on time, thank you for that.'

> 'Tom, I like the way you ignored that comment from Liam.'

Librarians mention other strategies for praising:

'I often target students who seem to have a bit of a label as badly behaved. If they come into the library at lunchtime I make a point of asking for their journal and writing a positive comment in it.'

'Giving rewards can be a sensitive business and in some situations I'm careful to draw a student to one side to praise them in case they feel embarrassed.'

'I have a dippers box with small treats in that I offer when students have gone out of their way to be particularly helpful or thoughtful.'

Reward yourself too

If we feel successful and believe we are valued we receive a boost to our self-esteem. This works for the pupils and it will work for the LRC staff too. Managing a busy fast moving environment such as an LRC is a tricky business, and managing students even more so. It can also be fairly isolating as you are not part of a large department which offers practical and emotional support and to which you can turn when the going gets tough.

Hopefully you will have a supportive line manager who will appreciate the work you do, support you during challenges and thank you when something has gone well. At the same time make sure you boost your own self esteem. Keep in touch with LRC colleagues in other schools; share success stories and pick each others' brains for valuable support. Keep your own log book in which you note down events or incidents that went well. These may well translate to useful material for a CV, and at the least they are a reminder of the good things which it is nice to look back on.

Give praise to colleagues too – don't simply grumble at their failures. We all like positive (but honest) feedback and this will help to develop a supportive atmosphere and better behaviour.

Sanctions

We have talked about rewards and the balance to these are sanctions. It is important to remember that behaviour management is *not* about punishments and confrontation. However, students need to know that if they choose to misbehave certain sanctions will automatically follow.

Ensure that pupils understand what will happen to them if they do not follow the expected code of behaviour. Wherever possible sanctions should operate as they do elsewhere in the school. If it is recommended that bad behaviour is reported to the form tutor in the first instance then that should be followed. It will help students to see that the same procedures are followed in the LRC as elsewhere in the school.

As a rule, sanctions should:

- Be simple and easy to uphold

- Operate in stages

- Be diagnostic. It is essential that pupils understand why their behaviour is unacceptable.

It may be tempting to respond to misbehaviour by banning the culprits from the LRC. While this may be an acceptable sanction it should be used sparingly, for a short period of time, and preferably as a last resort. If pupils are automatically sent out of the library as a way of dealing with every misdemeanour, this becomes less effective and no sanctions remain in reserve. If use of the LRC is regarded as pleasurable and important, then withdrawal of the privilege will be viewed as a serious punishment. It should be reserved for serious breaches, such as major disruption which is affecting other users.

Because exclusion from the LRC is a major sanction, it is important to reinforce this with students.

- Speak to them outside the LRC and make it clear why they have been sent out.

- Warn them that misbehaviour in the future will result in a longer withdrawal of the privilege.

- Enlist the support of pupils' form tutors by reporting the behaviour. This will demonstrate a united front. Ask them to reinforce the message.

- It may also be useful to obtain the head's permission to send a note home to parents/carers about the problems and the exclusion – which will only usually be allowed during non-teaching time.

Do have a look at Appendix 3.

Do remember too that you have a duty of care towards all your students and it is essential that you are aware of child protection policies that operate in your school. You may well see students at quieter times of the day, before or after school when few colleagues and other students may be about. Make sure that the parents know of any after school LRC activities in which their off spring are involved.

For more advice on managing specific incidents and individual pupils, see Section Three.

Section Three: General Strategies

Good behaviour is learned. We all have a responsibility to teach it and model it.

'All of us learn by watching and observing and then trying to copy... by modelling what you want pupils to do, you are setting them up to succeed. Pupils, like you and me, want to succeed; it inspires confidence in themselves.' [12]

The least effective way to manage behaviour is to tell a student what he or she is doing wrong. As we have already said behaviour management is not about punishment and confrontation; rather it is about letting students know what you expect of them and then helping them to succeed.

When you are managing a busy LRC during lunch time, break or indeed in a lesson, your own behaviour is the place to start. It is usually impossible to control other people's behaviour, and if we try we are setting ourselves up for failure. The most we are likely to do with this approach is create a climate of fear, alarm and resentment. The way forward is to learn how to modify our behaviour. If we aim for assertive rather than aggressive techniques we are more likely to manage behaviour successfully. We are aiming for a positive influence, not absolute control, and respect rather than fear and mistrust. We have already mentioned that adults who are usually glum and feel particularly stressed are more likely to allow feelings of hostility to show in their body language. This can immediately transfer to students, thus making them respond in an equally hostile way.

Aim to be assertive rather than aggressive. Features of assertive behaviour include:

- Standing back to review a tricky situation before getting involved

- Keeping calm and controlling one's temper

- Listening to all parties

- Keeping the discussion on a positive footing and talking about the problem not the pupil

- Making no negative personal comments

- Making sure everyone comes out of the situation with no serious loss of face. 'Put downs' don't provide long term solutions.

[12] Dunn, Roger. *Do's and Don'ts of Behaviour Management.*

Ask Yourself 'Why?'

All of us at some point will have to deal with misbehaviour. It is not a case of if so much as when! It will help considerably in our dealings with pupils if we can understand why they misbehave. At least one of the following factors is likely to be present.

Environmental Factors. It may be too hot or cold in the LRC, too noisy or too crowded. We all respond better when working in a comfortable environment. It may not be possible to alter the environment, but we should at least be aware of it and work towards making it as conducive as possible.

Social Factors. Students may be in a stressful situation at home. Something may have happened at school, perhaps a problem in a previous lesson, or a fall out with a friend. Again all of us are prone to 'off' days when things go wrong and we feel upset or annoyed. Students are no different and while this may not excuse bad behaviour it will go some way to explaining it. As adults we need to be aware of these possibilities as a reason why a student may fly off the handle or get upset or otherwise get into trouble.

Attention Seeking. This can happen in a lesson and during students' free time. If in a lesson it may be that they cannot cope with the task or the resources and demonstrate this by misbehaving. They may have low self esteem and difficulties with relationships which means the only way they know how to gain attention is by behaving badly. Again this may be a difficult problem to resolve, but an awareness of it will help to determine your reaction to it.

Being a Teenager! The teenage years bring about huge changes, both physical and mental. Indeed Nicola Morgan in *Blame My Brain*[13] points out that physical changes to the brain during adolescence are probably greater than at any other time apart from in very early childhood These are young people who are expected to act like adults, want to express themselves as young people and are often treated like children. They are learning how to change from being dependent physically, socially, economically and materially on their family group to becoming independent young people who are dealing with pressures to succeed at school, to earn money and to create a positive identity in their peer group.

> *'I used to take misbehaviour very much to heart and felt it was a personal attack on me. It's helped a lot to stop and ask myself why it is happening and to act accordingly. I have far fewer problems with behaviour management now because I have learnt to read situations better, to pre-empt problems and to laugh about some of the difficulties afterwards.'*

We are there to help our students to become adults, so patience and forgiveness can be really important to our relationship with our users.

---

[13] Morgan (2005) *Blame My Brain.*

Words...
Words...
Words...

We can't control our young people by force unless there is a life and death issue, so:

'Language is the most important tool we have when managing the behaviour of pupils.'

This is what many people believe' but psychologists tell us that it's not as simple as that. The *way* that you say something is far more meaningful than the words that you use. The graph of impact shows this.

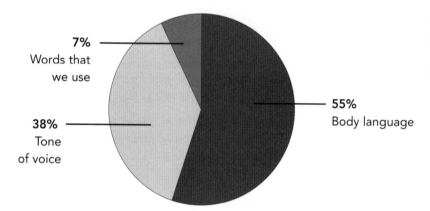

7%
Words that
we use

38%
Tone
of voice

55%
Body language

That doesn't mean to say that the words that we use aren't important, but they are only important in the context of other factors.

Using Language Positively

Consider the following statements:

'Well done, Anna. I can see that you have worked really hard on that homework. I'm sure your teacher will be very pleased.'

'Anna, you've been on that computer for nearly an hour and you've hardly done anything. What a waste of time.'

It's easy to see which of those statements will make the student feel understood and approved of. And it is easy to see the influence that language can have in either nurturing and supporting or hindering and wounding.

Only Link the Student with Good Behaviour

Be careful not to link the bad behaviour to the pupil as in 'You are very rude, Naveed.' It is far more effective to comment on the behaviour not the child. For example, the remark 'Naveed, you spoke rudely to Emma just now...' does not belittle the student, but makes it absolutely clear which behaviour is unacceptable.

Alternatively, when students do well and earn praise it is desirable to link that good behaviour with the student. Offering praise such as 'You are really thoughtful, Jenny' approves of the student as well as their behaviour and helps to build up a positive self image.

Use Positives Rather than Negatives

A comment such as: 'You're not using that encyclopaedia properly', is off-putting and reinforces a student's negative self image: 'I never do anything right...' whereas an alternative phrase 'I can help you use the encyclopaedia to find the information you need...' stops the student from feeling stupid or at fault and emphasises your role as a supportive adult who is there to help.

Use the Language of Choice

We all make choices about our own behaviour and your role as LRC staff is to help students make the right choice and ensure that they understand the consequences of their actions should they make the wrong choice. It is simple to put into practice and can be a very powerful tool. For example:

> 'Deborah, if you continue annoying Carl you will be choosing to sit on your own.'

> 'Michael, if you carry on disrupting this game you will be choosing to leave the LRC.'

By using the language of choice you are emphasising that the student is in charge of their own behaviour and you are also making clear what consequences will follow should they choose to continue with that behaviour.

The language of choice also removes that power struggle that can wear out any adult. In a power struggle you feel you have to make them behave and they are determined not to do as they are told. Tension is raised, nerves are jangled and tempers are frayed. Reminding students that they have a choice over their behaviour means that if they choose to misbehave, the resulting sanction is also their choice.

Obviously the language of choice needs to be balanced otherwise it could be a never ending series of negatives, 'you've chosen this... therefore this will happen.' It is important to balance this method with 'catch them being good' – praising them whenever they are working well and behaving as you would wish them to. Remember too that the language of choice can also be used positively:

> 'You chose to work on your project really well this lunch time, Melanie, well done.'

> 'I am really impressed that you've chosen to have a game of chess with Tanvir, Ben, well done.'

Using the when/then sentences can be really useful too:

> 'When you have finished tidying up, Y7s, then we'll finish off that exciting story that we started last week.'

'It wasn't me!' Avoiding an Argument

When pupils are caught doing something wrong they feel guilty – we all do! To feel better, a common ruse is to deflect responsibility, almost without thinking, so that we are hit with a barrage of arguments 'It wasn't me...', 'But I was only...', 'They were doing it too...' We as adults get drawn into this which creates more annoyance and frustration for us and shows to the pupils that their scam to deflect responsibility is actually working quite successfully!

The trick is to not get drawn into these dialogues. They only occur because the student is uncomfortable at being 'found out' and wants to make him/herself feel better. One solution is to use 'maybe...and' to diffuse the argument and return to the original problem.

For example:

'James you know you are not permitted on ring-tone sites, you must come off the site immediately.'

'But I was only looking up something for my cousin.'

'Maybe and I'd like you off that site straight away.'

'But Mr. Jones lets us go on them.'

'Maybe and I'd like you to come off that site and use the computer for something more constructive. Thank you.'

Walk away and allow a couple of minutes for take up time. If on your return James is working on something more acceptable thank him and move on. If he is still refusing to budge, it is time to use the language of choice:

'James you are choosing to continue on the ring-tone site and by doing so you are choosing to come off the computer.'

This means that you have put responsibility for the behaviour firmly in James' hand and you have opted for a sanction appropriate to the misbehaviour.

We all tend to use secondary behaviours on occasions. As adults we tend to provide rather lame excuses – the favourite is perhaps 'I didn't have time' or 'I forgot' when in fact you didn't like the task, or couldn't face it for any number of reasons. Children and young people tend to use physical methods too – they refuse to make eye contact with you or they stare at the ground or turn their head away. Advice is always to go for the primary behaviour problem – the reason for your initial interaction with them rather than argue about the secondary behaviour.

Use Positive Body Language

- Stand relaxed but upright, with your feet slightly apart.
- Avoid moving your head around. Concentrate.
- Look at the pupil concerned and if possible look into his/her eyes.
- Try to keep your eyes from looking downwards.
- Use positive hand gestures and open body language.
- Try to show a relaxed face and try to smile when appropriate.

Aim to be consistent

This isn't always easy when there are so many variables, and when we are all only human. However it is unfair on the pupils and damaging to your credibility to tackle misbehaviour one day and ignore (and thus condone) exactly the same action the next day. The inconsistency will confuse. They will doubt your judgement and probably accuse you of favouritism and of being 'unfair' – a common criticism levelled by teenagers at most adults.

But, and it is a big but… it's acceptable, indeed vital to deal with each situation as it arises. Your approach with each pupil will vary according to your knowledge of them, their age, past record etc and you won't always react to the same behaviour in different pupils. We are after all trying to get all pupils to a similar standard of courtesy and awareness of others but not necessarily by the same route.

Some of your students may feel this is unfair, but they must be prepared to trust you. You know best how to handle each situation.

Take time to weigh up a situation

Try to approach it quietly and calmly, allowing yourself time to appraise what is happening. Sometimes just standing and watching for a moment will make pupils acutely aware that you are there and they will immediately stop whatever they are doing. It gives you time to think and weigh your options too.

Avoid empty threats

If you warn pupils of the consequences of their actions, it is vital to follow this through. For example 'Leanne, by continuing to disturb and annoy Jayesh you are choosing for me to speak to your form tutor about your behaviour.' It is vital that you do just that, and that the pupil knows this will happen. Nothing will undermine your authority more quickly than a threat which cannot be kept or which you do not follow through.

Deal with the problem away from friends and spectators

When groups are in the LRC, you may come across a student misbehaving for the entertainment of his or her friends. Firstly identify and if possible remove the ringleader from the group and deal with the behaviour at a distance from the others. If this isn't possible – often the ring leader is the most difficult to deal with, then deal with one of the others and see the leader later away from the group (or even a gang). This may mean calling for him/her out of a different lesson.

Make them come to you

If you see misbehaviour in a distant part of the LRC, rather than rushing to the scene, call the pupils to you. This immediately exerts your authority and the length of time it takes pupils to walk to you will often calm them down and help diffuse the situation. Always give waiting time and never belittle a young person by demanding instant obedience.

Think 'Why' not 'What'

Behaviour is communicating a need and it will help to deal with the behaviour problem if you can become attuned to why a student is misbehaving. We have already mentioned that a number of factors may cause behaviour problems (see Ask Yourself 'Why?' p.27). During an LRC lesson it may be that the student is not comfortable with the task or the resources; this could easily manifest itself in disruptive behaviour. It is then tempting to tackle the behaviour without combating the underlying cause. If you have paused to ask yourself 'why?' you are more likely to be able to resolve the situation satisfactorily.

Allow Take-up time

If you have asked a pupil to do something, especially if you have commented on inappropriate behaviour and asked them to change it, don't expect an instant response. If possible move away and allow the pupil time to comply. Those couple of minutes take the pressure off and give a bit of face saving to the pupil. You can always return if the problem persists.

Never stand over a student waiting impatiently for them to comply with your instruction. This is the quickest way to a direct confrontation from which nobody wins.

Aim to tackle a problem when you feel calm

If you feel angry or upset and tired, then you are unlikely to think clearly, and therefore unlikely to react, rationally. Appearing calm reduces the likelihood of conflict and allows the problem to be resolved more easily, so take the heat out of the situations. Make the pupil wait in a quiet corner of the LRC or in your office, if you have one. Do something else for a few minutes until your anger abates, and remember that this also allows pupils to calm down and think about what they have done. It doesn't matter if this also gives them time to think up an excuse, because you will simply use 'maybe, and' (see Use the Language of Choice p.29) to pin point the main problem. If you still feel upset, or if the incident is serious, now is the time to request assistance from another member of staff.

We're not trying to say it's easy....

Managing behaviour is not easy, especially in a stressful and confrontational situation which was perhaps none of your making in the first place. Patience, practice and persistence are all needed. All these strategies can work, but they will take practice. Practise some of these ideas in small steps and in different situations. It's useful to remember, although not always easy, that you're trying to develop these pupils' behavioural and social skills and not simply trying to 'control' them. It's also helpful to remember that you are the adult in these difficult situations and that you are modelling and teaching the behaviour that is acceptable and which makes the LRC a pleasant place to be for everyone, both staff and pupils!

Specific strategies can be adopted in various circumstances such as managing student behaviour during a lesson in the LRC, during free time in the LRC and when individuals or small groups use the LRC.

Using the LRC during lessons

The LRC will inevitably be used to support the curriculum. Librarians and teachers alike acknowledge the value of a learning pathway which allows pupils to develop the skills needed to find, organise, evaluate and present information and thus become independent learners.

When it works this kind of learning exemplifies the partnerships between teacher, LRC staff and students. When teacher and LRC staff work in harmony, confident in their respective roles, students respond to the positive input of both, and a relaxed, yet purposeful learning atmosphere is apparent. As already mentioned, you as the librarian, are in a unique position within a school: not a teacher, yet closely involved with students and their learning. You can ensure that your LRC offers the kind of environment where students are more likely to behave appropriately, remain on task and therefore learn successfully.

To make this happen two things are crucial:

- A good relationship between teacher and LRC staff
- An effective learning atmosphere in the Library Resources Centre.

Building Bridges — the Relationship between Teacher and LRC Staff

Before the teacher brings a class into the library you are likely to be thinking about a number of issues:

- Has the teacher shared his/her lesson planning and objectives with you?
- Does the teacher understand your expertise?
- The teacher is not on his/her territory, but should the rules of the classroom still apply?
- To what extent will pupils be permitted to behave differently because they are not in the classroom?
- If a pupil misbehaves, should the librarian intervene or leave it to the teacher? Who should intervene first?
- How and when should LRC staff offer help and guidance to pupils?

It is essential that these questions are asked and debated so that LRC staff and teacher can work effectively together. If they remain unanswered students will quickly pick up on any problems and behaviour is more likely to degenerate, making the teacher think twice about using the LRC in future and undermining the confidence of LRC staff.

The best way to avoid this scenario is to plan in advance. The teacher is coming into your territory and a bit of forward planning allows both parties to identify an appropriate role. In this situation the role of LRC staff has a particular advantage. The teacher must have a constant overview of the activities and progress of the whole class, while you, in a supportive role, can concentrate fully on one student or a small group for as long as necessary. Forward planning should even provide the opportunity to identify which pupils would most benefit from your attention. By being well organised, supportive and interested you are demonstrating just how much the LRC has to offer. Devise your own checklist of questions (or invite the teacher to complete a simple booking form) and discuss them with the teacher before the LRC session. Remember too that this information will be very useful indeed as part of your self-evaluation processes.

- How many pupils will be coming?
- Are you likely to have individuals or small groups from other classes already present?
- Will the class have any other support from teaching assistants?
- Is this a one-off lesson or part on an extended project in the LRC?
- Which skills are the focus? Finding information, notemaking, presenting information, independent study, team work?
- What kind of activities will be taking place? Can resources be prepared beforehand?
- How will you be supporting the activities? Demonstrating use of a new website? Helping students to search the internet? Helping their research in encyclopaedias, atlases or statistics?
- Who will organise the clearing away at the end of the session?

Once you have planned the LRC lesson, are familiar with the objectives and have identified your role, the lesson can go ahead. Now is the time to get the students into the LRC, settle them down in an environment crackling with interest, enthusiasm and hard work. Although LRC staff often play a largely supportive role, real partnership working is useful and stimulating to teacher and librarian. The students are in your territory and there is a great deal you can do to promote an atmosphere that is calm, relaxed and purposeful. Effective strategies can be adopted even before the lesson begins.

Whenever possible:

- Prepare resources in advance.
- Be ready to welcome pupils when they arrive.
- Greet them at the door and find out one or two first names.
- Tell them where you want them to sit.
- Ask them to get pencil cases, journals, etc. out of their bags and sit

quietly. Thank one or two as they do this. Such reinforcement encourages the message to filter to all pupils.

- As soon as the teacher arrives, expect him or her to take control. The class belongs to the teacher, not to you, and your supportive role should already have been agreed.

'I don't understand!'

'I'm not being naughty; this is me telling you that I don't understand!'

The main purpose of using the LRC within the curriculum is to give students the opportunity to work independently and take greater responsibility for what and how they learn. Pupils now have more freedom to make decisions about their work, but on the downside more is expected of them which can lead to confusion or uncertainty. To learn successfully these students need to be motivated, persistent, methodical, self aware and good at working independently, yet equally capable of working as part of a team. The level of maturity demanded can make it difficult for them to cope and behaviour problems are often a reaction to this.

'I've noticed one or two students wandering aimlessly looking for a pencil when really this is just avoidance. They're confused and need help in getting started.'

'It's important not to make assumptions. I had some year 7 students looking up Charles Dickens under C. They were so frustrated at not finding any information they gave up. A short lesson on using encyclopaedias solved the problem!'

'During planning with the teacher we identified one pupil who would do everything possible to get sent out of the room. We felt this was because he was anxious about not being able to complete the work. We teamed him up with two other students and I spent all lesson with the three of them modelling, explaining and encouraging. That boy stayed in the lesson and left with a smile on his face!'

Students with Special Needs

We all know that over the past decade there is a growing trend for mainstream schools to be more inclusive and for students with Special Needs to be warmly welcomed and accommodated wherever possible. This has brought more responsibility to library staff who should be aware of these students, their needs and how to interact with them. We have already stated that it is essential for all library staff, in line with other colleagues in school, to have knowledge of students with difficulties, whatever they may be. This ensures that they can provide the care and attention necessary when these pupils are using the library during both curriculum and non-curriculum time. It is also possible that due to their challenges these students may be bullied. Managing the behaviour of some of these students – especially those with

Autism, Spectrum Disorder (ASD), including Asperger's Syndrome and also Attention Deficit Hyperactivity Disorder (ADHD) – needs more patience, knowledge and training. (See the list of Further Reading in Appendix 4.) It is estimated that approximately 1% of the school population experience autism and up to 5% show ADHD symptoms. Many students are not diagnosed and have no personal statement and direct support in schools.

To help these students it is generally a good idea to:

- Talk to the SENCO to learn of the latest information about particular students and strategies being used by teaching staff
- Seat the student with a mentor from the same year group who can act as a positive role model
- Provide activities of a visual and kinaesthetic nature
- Give very clear bite-size instructions
- Provide help with time management and personal organisation of work, files etc.
- Encourage the use of personal checklists to support organisation and meeting deadlines
- Allow physical movement around the room if possible, movement that is work-focused
- Use positive feedback and rewards rather than the threat of sanctions
- Use 'time out' strategies to reduce stress – not as any sort of punishment
- Remember that the behaviour with which you are coping usually isn't of your making.

Delivering a Lesson

When the LRC is used within the curriculum, the LRC staff's role is usually supportive. There may, however, be occasions, for example during LRC induction, when LRC staff take full responsibility for a class and the accompanying teacher has the supporting role. The teacher will be present and involved in the activities, but it is the LRC staff that plan and deliver the lesson. You must be able to capture interest, control behaviour and teach a class with differing abilities and unique personalities. While the content of the lesson is extremely important, the way in which it is delivered is equally so, as the techniques adopted can directly influence the behaviour of the group and therefore the success of the lesson. It is important to:

- Decide on the activities and the order in which they will be carried out.
- Consider room layout and organise materials in advance.
- Remember that not everyone has to do the same activities in the same order. Working their way around a series of work stations can be interesting and motivating for pupils, especially kinaesthetic learners.

- Plan a variety of tasks including some which allow students to work in a small group or with a partner.
- Give clear instructions. Ensure everyone is seated and facing you before talking to the class as a whole.
- As you begin to speak, make eye contact and draw pupils into the lesson.
- Get them involved as soon as possible. Ask questions to keep their interest and to confirm their understanding.
- Use positive body language.

'I give a talk on the library database for year 11 GNVQ students. I've developed a PowerPoint presentation to keep their interest and I always make sure that part of the session gives them the chance to test out the database for themselves by using the catalogue.'

'When I am doing my induction session for year 7, I give them a quiz to complete which means they have to leave their seat and explore the LRC. They always enjoy it and it gives them a break from sitting and listening.'

Small Group Management

On occasions an individual or a small group may need to use the LRC during a lesson. These sessions are often unplanned and arise from the need to find something out or pursue further research.

Students will respond to this opportunity in various ways. Some will be keen and interested; others will be uncertain about what they need to do, and some may view it as an excuse to avoid working and fool around. The LRC staff may already be involved with a different lesson, in which case the reason for the visit to the LRC needs to be identified and help given speedily and effectively.

This type of LRC use will be more informal, so it may be helpful to remind pupils that their time should be spent purposefully. Arrange beforehand that students using the LRC in this way always bring a research slip from their teacher, giving the name of the pupil(s), the question(s) being researched – not simply the topic under investigation (this is poor information literacy teaching) – and it could include the length of time to be spent in the LRC. This is a vital link between teacher, pupil and LRC staff. Copies of these research slips can also be used again as part of the library's self-evaluation process. It ensures that the relationship between student and LRC staff is meaningful, and discourages teachers who may be looking for a reason to get rid of someone for a few minutes! Teachers may argue that they are short of time but students who don't arrive with a research slip can be asked politely to return to their class. The message will soon get around.

Sometimes pupils will arrive without a research slip and/or without pen or paper. Do not grumble, but send them back to fetch equipment and a note. This may seem petty and time-wasting, but the message will reach both teacher and pupil that bringing the right equipment to the LRC encourages the right frame of mind and therefore the appropriate behaviour – showing interest, commitment and enthusiasm. If lack of equipment or a note becomes a real problem it may be worth reminding teachers of what you expect via a staff bulletin or via the intranet.

Once pupils have arrived in the LRC, use the slip as a basis to find out more.

- Ask them to tell you what they need to find out. This allows you to check that they understand the purpose of their visit.

- Check that they know how to find and use resources.

- If you have time to assess their competence, ask them to talk you through how they will use the information in front of them.

- Encourage them to come to you if they get stuck and check on them occasionally to make sure they are on task.

- Encourage all the pupils to work independently, but also let them know that help is available. This delicate balance will help give them the motivation to pursue their work without becoming distracted.

Free Time

When the LRC is used during free time, several issues need to be considered.

- This is students' own time when they want to be more relaxed and enjoy themselves.

- A mix of students, ages and abilities is likely to be present.

- The LRC will be used for a variety of purposes.

Firstly and most importantly, make a conscious decision about the activities you feel are acceptable in your LRC. These may be all or some of the following:

- Homework
- Reading
- Borrowing and returning books
- Active research: Locating useful resources

  Finding out

  Note-taking
- ICT facilities: Internet

  School Intranet/VLE
- Board Games, puzzles and brain teasers.

LRC staff want pupils to enjoy the LRC during their free time, but this is tempered with the need for it to be used as a library and not as a common room or meeting place. The way in which pupils are permitted to use the LRC at lunch time and after school will influence both their opinions of the LRC and the library staff and their behaviour while they are there.

> 'When I first came here the library had not been open much because of staffing problems and it was like the Marie Celeste at lunch times. To try and drum up support I went round form rooms during registration to show off new books and talk about the services we had to offer. It did the trick and now I'm consistently busy.

> 'The LRC used to be really quiet after school so I started up a reading group and we now meet regularly and have just started shadowing this year's Carnegie medal shortlist.

> 'Our school has a sixth form and many of them use the LRC for study purposes. It can be quite difficult to balance that with younger pupils who want to relax with a game of Boggle during break or lunch. As a compromise we offer games during two lunch times a week and that seems to work effectively.'

> 'I introduced chess, draughts and Mastermind as break and lunch activities. That was fine until some students decided the library would be a good place to play cards. I nipped that in the bud very quickly and explained that only educational games provided by the library could be played in the library!'

During lunch time and after school LRC staff are likely to be working on their own with a large number of students to supervise. To retain your good humour and ensure that everything runs smoothly, consider adopting the following strategies:

Keep an overview. Your role during free time is to have an overview of everything that is going on, so it may be impossible to devote yourself entirely to one pupil or one enquiry. When helping a student, position yourself so that you can see what is going on and scan the LRC frequently.

> 'I find it quite frustrating not being able to spend as much time as I would like helping a pupil, but so many are demanding help that you have to spread yourself thinly. One solution I came up with was to keep an enquiry book in which I log the enquiry and the name of the student so that I can go back to it when I have more time.'

Develop a presence. Avoid sitting at a desk. Aim to be on the move so that pupils know you are around. Get involved with the pupils, chat with them and ask what they are doing. You may need to make yourself heard above a babble of voices, so practise projecting your voice as an alternative to shouting. Lower your voice when speaking more loudly and it will travel further with less strain.

> *'I try to avoid queues and crowds anywhere as that's often a flashpoint for behaviour problems, for example I won't allow any 'hangers on' around the ICT equipment. The rule is one person per computer otherwise crowds congregate and trouble is never far behind!'*

Get to know the pupils. This is not always easy, especially when you see large numbers only occasionally, but getting to know students makes your job more fulfilling and demonstrates to the students that you are interested in them as individuals.

> *'I'm fortunate to be blessed with a good memory for names, but I also like to learn about the students, their thoughts and interests. It's nice to know who goes to karate, who's got a new kitten, who's mum is about to have a baby. It gives you a basis on which to relate to them and it makes managing them that much easier.'*

Avoid over-familiarity. Do not fall into the trap of treating pupils as friends and equals as they may try to take advantage of friendly overtures which will lead to confusion and problems. Always retain a professional distance and aim for a relaxed and pleasant relationship, while not allowing pupils to push the boundaries too far.

Appoint LRC Assistants. Train students to work on the desk and carry out basic housekeeping duties like issuing and returning books. This will free you to move around the LRC and become involved in the activities of those using it. (See SLA Guideline, *Organising Voluntary Help in the School Library*, details in Appendix 4, or the *Pupil Librarian Toolkit* on the SLA website.)

> *'During lunch time my student LRC helpers run the library counter which gives me a chance to be moving around the library checking who needs help and keeping an eye open for any problems.'*

Involve Your Students — Student Voice

Appointing LRC assistants is just one way of getting the students involved. There are others. Making decisions about the physical environment is one such area. The LRC layout, displays and resources are good places to begin. By consulting your customers you are more likely to have an LRC which reflects their needs and interests. This in turn can influence the students' perceptions of the LRC and their behaviour in it. They cannot expect to be consulted over every decision, but why not consider some of the following:

- Allow students to be involved in stock selection, for example giving them a set amount to be spent on popular fiction

- Appoint voluntary helpers. (for more on this see the SLA Guideline *Organising Voluntary Help in the School Library* or the *Pupil Librarian Toolkit* on the SLA website)

- If major changes to layout are anticipated, display plans and ask for suggestions and feedback

- Hold a termly meeting with representatives from each year group to put forward ideas and suggestions

- Use the LRC as a base for student mentoring and buddy activities

- Develop links with your School Council

- Involve students in running clubs and activities such as homework clubs or reading groups

- Involve students in promotional activities such as book fairs and author visits.

We know that in lots of schools where students lack social space, the library can become very overcrowded. In some schools the senior management team is happy to see the library soak up any pupils who wish to visit as this reduces pressure elsewhere, especially that of the lunchtime supervisors. LRC staff can become little more than child minders. This attitude is clearly unsatisfactory. It is important to retain the LRC ethos at all times – if the users cannot use the facilities effectively due to excess noise and distraction and pressure of numbers then policies need to be rethought.

In extreme circumstances it might be reasonable to close the LRC at lunchtime in order to avoid misuse. Perhaps the key problem appears to be misuse of library ICT facilities – then we suggest it might be wise to close them down at lunchtimes. They can be freely used only when direct supervision and support is available – probably during lesson time and before and after school.

Section Five: Whole School Approaches

The LRC staff should be involved in all aspects of training and coaching regarding behaviour management.

Virtually all the behaviour reports and advice in recent years have mentioned that all teaching and support staff should be involved in whole school behaviour discussions and training. This guideline offers ideas on promoting positive behaviour and tackling misbehaviour. Some of the suggestions will be useful to you, but others perhaps less applicable.

The value of whole school INSET on the other hand is that it is shaped to your particular school and its needs. There is something extremely morale boosting in attending such a session with your colleagues and knowing that this is a collective attempt to improve a situation; to come up with new ideas and to develop practices which are unique to your school and set in situations that will help all of you in your relationships with students.

It has been known for such INSET to be offered, but for LRC staff to somehow be overlooked, so that they don't get to hear about it, or it is considered 'unnecessary' for them to attend. Fortunately the impact of workforce reform means there are more support staff working directly with students than ever before. Any INSET should be open for you to attend; especially if it will have a direct impact on how you do your job.

The Steer Report recommends that INSET on behaviour management should be available for all staff and also emphasises that head teachers have a responsibility to lead from the front and that leadership to support positive behaviour must be shared across the whole staff, including support staff.

Whole school INSET is not the only way to receive training about behaviour management. Consider the following possibilities.

- A Buddy system – link up with a colleague from another school for support and to discuss behaviour issues and what works and what doesn't. You may find that they are using strategies which you would find useful too.

- Look out in the professional press for details of Behaviour Management courses. Your Schools Library Service and the School Library Association may also have details.

- Shadow a member of staff. If you work with a colleague who seems to manage behaviour issues particularly then pick their brains and ask if you can sit in on a lesson to observe their methods.

If you are new to a job it is even more important that training is given in managing pupils. It has already been mentioned in section one that LRC staff should make sure that they get to know the school policy on managing behaviour. As a new member of staff this should be part of your induction programme. This induction programme may be a formal affair conducted with other new members of staff, or it may be an informal session with your line manager. How it is presented is less important than the content, but if it is very informal it may be worth ensuring that the following areas are covered regarding behaviour.

As part of your induction you should be given a copy of the school's behaviour policy and it should make clear the following points.

- Which member(s) of senior staff have overall management of pastoral care and behaviour issues within the school.

- How the behaviour policy is put into action – Are there incident report forms to complete ? To whom is a behaviour problem reported in the first instance? How are sanctions increased if problems continue?

- Those students that have specific emotional and behavioural difficulties and details of these difficulties – you should have access to the same information as teaching staff. The SENCO maybe a useful contact here.

- The role of the head of year and form tutor in managing behaviour problems.

- The role of your line manager in supporting you when problems with behaviour arise.

Most schools take the induction process seriously, realising that to ensure confident and happy staff at ease within the school and in their own job everyone needs a period of orientation and support. After all it is in the school's interest that you follow procedures and are singing from the same hymn sheet. However, if you are unfortunate enough to join a school where for some reason the induction process is overlooked it is vital that you approach your line manager with a list of questions and pursue this until you are happy that you have the information you need to be able to do your job successfully.

Working with difficult adults

As we all know, not everyone in school has the same perceptions and attitudes to the library as the library staff. Everyone is focused on their own areas of responsibility and work. Everyone is usually very busy and sometimes lack of immediate concern for others and shortened thought processes and language can lead to misunderstanding. Typical tensions arises from:

- Senior management team members who brook no discussion and compromise about use of the library.

- Teaching colleagues who see themselves as superior to library staff and have a rather antiquated view of its users. They appear to believe that silence is the key to an effective library. These are just the people who jump about and loudly demand silence or grumble at noise levels when you are at your busiest, which appears to demean you.

- Line managers who don't have the time, inclination and knowledge to manage library staff effectively.

- Teaching colleagues who continually send students to the LRC for what you see as the wrong reasons.

- Teachers who seem to support the students rather than you and your priorities.

- Groups who book/use the LRC for meetings without a polite request to you and then perhaps leave the debris of the meeting to be cleared by you and your helpers, without even a 'thank you' sometimes.

- ICT staff who appear to give the library less priority for hardware and software problems.

- Support staff who use the LRC with small groups and appear to operate counter to your well honed policies and practices, in spite of your explanations and beseeching.

That of course isn't their attitude. They all (like the rest of us) see themselves as sensible people who are doing their best for the school as a whole and the student body at large. They don't see themselves as awkward, overbearing, rude and inconsiderate – none of us do!

Communication

So what's the answer? Basically it's better communication! The better you know your colleagues, trust their judgement and work in a team with them, the greater the understanding, camaraderie and the less friction there will tend to be. Yes there will be misunderstandings but not major friction. To become a part of a team and avoid tensions, it is important to:

- Mix freely with colleagues during occasional breaks and lunchtimes, meetings and social gatherings

- Publicise LRC policies, plans and events as openly and actively as possible to everyone so they respect and appreciate your role

- If you find yourself in a difficult situation turn in the first instance to your line manager for support and failing that to another senior member of staff

- If you have a complaint then put it in writing – sleep on it, check the facts and then ask for a response from the person to whom you are complaining

- Provide positive feedback to colleagues

- Avoid grumbles and try to offer solutions to problems

- Use all the same behaviour management techniques that you use with students

- Remember that *to have a friend you need to be a friend.*

Clearly we all have different perspectives of situations, but trust and communication go a long way to avoid the problems that many LRC staff appear to face on a regular basis.

A real difference

We all know that running an LRC is a fantastic job. We can make a real difference to learning and we can help produce readers for life and students who are more literate.

People who are more literate are happier, more likely to be in a lasting relationship and living in their own home.

Men in particular benefit, with 43 per cent of those with poor literacy – equal to a seven-year-old – living alone, compared to 30 per cent who have enough reading skills to attain a C or above in a GCSE, according to a study by the National Literacy Trust.

Almost a quarter of men – 22 per cent – who struggle with reading still live with their parents, compared with just 9 per cent of those with good literacy.

Just half of people who struggle with books claim to be "satisfied with life", compared with 78 per cent of those who can read well. Literate people also tend to be better paid and smoke less.[14]

Libraries are essential to the well being of effective schools.

However managing behaviour is by no means easy. It takes practice, perseverance and the realisation that it is impossible to get it right every time. Practise new strategies until you find what works for you and remember the importance of body language, tone of voice and language itself when managing students or dealing with difficult colleagues. Always remember that you are managing people not machines, and don't be too hard on yourself when things go wrong from time to time.

Remember that your contributions are helping to reinforce and develop the school ethos, helping to equip students with effective social skills and also helping you to realise your vision for the LRC. When the atmosphere is crackling with motivated students, hard at work and thoroughly enjoying every aspect of the LRC, don't forget to congratulate yourself, because you made it happen!

---

[14] *The Daily Telegraph* 13 September 2008.
http://www.telegraph.co.uk/news/2776516/Reading-makes-people-happier-and-more-successful-in-love.html

Cool, Calm and Collected

Case Studies

Laura Taylor

Librarian,
City of London Academy,
Southwark

City of London Academy, Southwark

City of London Academy in Southwark, London, is an 11–19 mixed Academy of 1,100 pupils, with approximately 100+ students in the Sixth Form.

I have worked in three inner city comprehensive schools and still have plenty to learn about managing students' behaviour in the school library but for what it is worth here are some of the experiences, negative and positive, I have had and some of the strategies I have picked up along the way.

I freely admit that there are times I have gone home in tears in the past and have spent sleepless nights worrying about the arguments I was having with some of the more challenging students in one school. I was letting things get to me. As a school librarian we are often on our own – handed the keys to the library and told to get on with it! There is not the support of a faculty or department with colleagues and a Head of Department who you can call on for support or advice when faced with a group of screaming teenage girls or marauding teenage boys at lunchtime in an overcrowded library. I have to admit to not being the calmest of people – I tend to let my emotions show – and have a temper (as friends, family and undoubtedly some colleagues and students will confirm). There are numerous occasions I have made mistakes and undoubtedly mishandled a situation and indeed made it worse by forgetting to maintain a professional approach. When a student is rude to me or behaves badly towards another student I can feel my hackles rise, the adrenalin begin to flow and all my natural instincts set me on the offensive!

So how was I going to deal with my own anger? As one trainer said on one of the courses I attended – 'You can't change students' behaviour, only your own and how you respond and deal with a situation.' I went on a couple of behaviour management courses, watched some Teachers TV videos by various behaviour management gurus (Bill Rogers, Paul Blum), talked to teaching colleagues and read some of the wealth of literature on classroom management techniques and anger management that I had in my staff library. Many of these ideas and strategies can be applied and adapted to a library although I think it is much harder in many ways as we don't have the benefit of seating plans, registers, a board where we can write up names of those behaving well and those behaving badly (apart from when we may have lessons in the library) – all strategies most teachers adopt.

In fact we operate in a very different context from the classroom and it is therefore sometimes difficult for students to understand what our expectations are. We have one set of expectations on their behaviour during lessons in the library, when the librarian and the teacher may be directing activities, and quite another during breaks and lunchtimes. Students are encouraged to wander around (we call it browsing!) but this can be easily confused by some students as meaning they can spend the whole hour aimlessly running around, or hiding books in other students' bags or pockets so as to set the security alarm off when they leave!

So these are some of the strategies I have adopted and adapted over the years.

- **Involve the students** – let them see that the library is a whole school resource and in fact their space which you manage and are in charge of on their behalf. Let them see it is in their interests for their peers to use it appropriately. Most of them will come to a sensible consensus about how they would like the library to be used and will agree with you on sanctions that should be applied to any miscreants. If you explain why there are certain rules they are more likely to accept them and support you. In one school I had huge issues with students continually playing games on the computers. I would have arguments with students over this but then enlisted the support of their peers who needed to use a computer for school work. I would tell a student that another needed the computer for their work and more often than not they would willingly come off their game playing and allow their peer to use it for legitimate work reasons. Ask for the library to be discussed at Student Council or recruit students representatives to look at behaviour issues in the library. Perhaps they can work with you on drawing up a code of behaviour?

- Then get students and library staff to sign a **joint agreement or contract** on what each should expect of the other. Ours outlines the facilities, services, resources and support we will offer to students in return for them recognising the code of conduct on display around the library. They sign this at the beginning of their school career and again in Year 12. Make this clear in their induction sessions and discuss what behaviour they think is appropriate and what sanctions should be applied to those who transgress.

- Have clear **visual signs** displayed around the library highlighting this code of behaviour and your expectations. I didn't want a lengthy list of negative 'Don'ts' on display but rather a short list of positives 'You are welcome to read, browse, study, borrow. If you wish to eat, drink, run around, or be noisy then please go to the playground' all illustrated with clear visuals. Keep these clear and simple or no-one will read them. Save the detail for a policy document. You can point to these signs and remind students of 'the rules'.

- **Welcome the students in to the library.** At lunchtimes I try and make a point of being at the door as we open up and allow the first 50 students, who have lined up outside, come in- just as I do at the beginning of a lesson. It is school policy and good behaviour management. I send out a clear message that I am in charge in this space and when they come in I expect they must have something constructive to do. At the same time I am building relationships with the students – getting to know them –

meeting and greeting. Often the hardest part is when they know you do not know their names and so will find it difficult to follow up on any misbehaviour. In some schools you can ask to see a student's planner or lunchcard, or you may be able to check photos on the library or school management system. As I wander around the library helping and advising students whilst keeping an ever watchful eye (it helps to have eyes in the back of your head of course!) I soon spot the one or two who are invariably 'up to no good' so I let them know I know they are here with a friendly greeting, and maybe a positive suggestion on something they might like to look at: 'Seen the new *Guinness Book of Records*?'; 'Have you seen that new film yet – we've got the book it was based on if you are interested.'

■ **Decide on what you are prepared to manage.** If the library is noisy and chaotic and you are on your own effectively managing and supervising 100 students (yes – I have been there!) then limit numbers. No teacher would be expected to work with 100 students on their own. You are not there to manage crowd control or supervise you are there to support and advise students on their reading choices and their homework. There are various ways of doing this – issuing library passes, limiting entry to specific year groups on specific days or, as I did, liaise with a Head of Year and get prefects timetabled to manage the door and allow only a specified number of students at a time into the library. Ultimately you really need more adult support – either from a rota of teachers or a Head of Year on patrol as well as additional staff actually in the library. If you are fortunate enough to have a supportive Head, as I do, they will recognise the value of what you do and how the work you are doing increases the popularity and demand on the library hence the need for additional staff. We now always have two library staff timetabled for break and lunchtimes with the back up of a team of Year assistants on patrol around school should things escalate. Whatever you decide ensure that this is written into a policy and that all staff and particularly senior management are made aware of how many students you will supervise. There are clear Health and Safety issues involved here and you need to ensure you are covered and supported.

■ Use well known behaviour management techniques – the broken record technique. Repeat instructions; don't personalise an issue or make personal remarks about a student – refer to the behaviour that is inappropriate not the individual themselves; think about what you want to achieve – and make that clear to them; clearly state what they are doing and what you would like them to do: 'I can see you have a lot of energy to burn off but I'd like you to sit down and stop disturbing other students'; give them a choice and don't back them into a corner or make them lose face or humiliate them in front of their peers. 'Ok if you can sit down and get on with something you are welcome to stay but if you want to run around I will have to ask you to leave'; be specific – don't tell them they are a pain in the neck (even though they always are!) but refer to the particular behaviour or incident that is of concern; don't get drawn into an argument; don't apologise – after all you are the adult and in charge of the library; be polite, confident, in control, consistent, professional and firm but fair. They are entering your space and must abide by your rules; give the student a warning and choices. Finally follow up and mean what you say otherwise they will be back tomorrow having seen they can wind you up with no repercussions for them!

- **Make these policies clear to staff.** It is important that teaching staff are also made aware of how students are expected to behave in the library particularly when bringing in a class. Ensure you include this information in staff handbooks and in any INSET or information you give to new staff. This might include how students should be expected to line up at the door until the teacher arrives, how the teacher is responsible for a class's behaviour during a lesson, and how a class will tidy up and be dismissed from the library at the end of the lesson. Clarifying such issues ensures any conflict of roles between library staff and teachers is avoided. We all have had the unfortunate experience of a teacher who sees the 'library lesson' as a chance to catch up on marking, read a magazine or absolve all responsibility for a class. Emphasise to staff how you are aiming to achieve a team-teaching approach and wish to work co-operatively with your teaching colleagues in relation to class management.

- **Reward good behaviour!** Library staff at my school have merit stamps and can reward students for good work and behaviour just as teaching staff do. We also have a system of sending memos to tutors and Heads of Year commenting on good behaviour and send postcards home to parents praising students who have worked well or helped out in the library in some way. We regularly give all students an opportunity to help out in the library as library assistants and particularly encourage those who may have displayed more challenging behaviour to re-direct their energies in a more positive direction often with surprising results. Many of the students who are disruptive in the library are often repeating a pattern of negative behaviour around the school. If we can raise their self esteem, by giving them a positive role to play in school life through taking on a role in the library it can impact on their whole school behaviour.

- **Take deep breaths**, keep calm and don't lose your temper! Easier said than done I know. Someone once said I should pretend I am wearing a suit of armour and not let any personal jibes affect me. I should walk away and count to 10 before dealing with a situation – again not always easy or appropriate if an incident has just happened and the perpetrator is on their way out of the door!

- **Get help!** Get hold of the school's behaviour management policy (there should be one) and find out how the system works in your school. Liaise with whoever is responsible for behaviour in your school – tutors, Heads of Year, pastoral teams etc. Follow up on any incidents immediately using whatever systems are in place. Talk to colleagues – you will find the students giving you a hard time are doing the same everywhere in school and so don't take it personally. Teachers will give you helpful tips and practical advice of strategies they use in the classroom. I have access to SIMS so can enter any concerns after the incident and it will be followed up by Heads of Years and tutors in the next day or so.

■ **Follow and apply the school's code of behaviour** and apply the same sanctions and rewards as the teaching staff. Students need to see the library as applying the same expectations as teachers do in the classroom. All members of staff – support and otherwise – are entitled to the same respect. If mobile phones are not allowed in the school then that includes the library. If food and drink is limited to the dining hall than that means there should be no eating or drinking in the library (well – we can all make exceptions for the odd book group or library helper party can't we!)

■ **Attend any INSET** on behaviour management you can, whether internal or external.

Just remember **it takes time**. Get involved in school life – talk to the students outside the library – if you see them at lunch or in the playground smile, stop and say hello and have a chat. Make sure you are regarded and treated by students with the same respect and in the same way as the teaching staff. All the surveys of students' opinion of teachers (and by extension all school staff) indicates that they don't like staff who shout but they do like staff who are firm but fair and consistent and have a sense of humour. Students see me at assemblies, talking, sitting and eating with the teaching staff – most of them call me a teacher. All staff are expected to apply the school rules on behaviour, uniform etc around the school. As librarians we are lucky in being able to have a slightly different relationship with students – after all we don't tend to have to set homework, mark tests, write reports etc. and whilst we can and should be friendly we can never be their friend. I remember all too well, when I was very much younger, making that mistake early on and letting them call me by my first name. It threw the younger kids so I soon reverted to being 'Mrs King' (my maiden name) – most disconcerting for me as that was my Mum!)

Remember students are out to test any new member of staff – but gradually you will build up relationships with them, get to know their names and see them as individuals – then maybe they will see you one as one too! And remember most of them will grow out of it – I have had many a laugh reminiscing with 6th formers about what a pain they were in the dreaded Year 9!

Case Study 2: The Emmbrook School

Barbara Band

*Head of Library and Resources
The Emmbrook School,
Berkshire*

The Emmbrook School

The Emmbrook School in Berkshire is an 11–18 mixed comprehensive of 1,200+ students with 200 in the Sixth Form.

Background

The school has a 'managing behaviour for learning' policy that is regularly updated, with positive attitude towards learning characteristics drawn up by the student council. This sets down behaviour expectations both inside and outside the classroom, focusing on positive actions, with appropriate rewards and sanctions applicable. All staff are expected to apply this policy ensuring that behaviour management is clear and consistent. Rewards can be given individually and include verbal, written, merits, commendations and letters home, or they can be given for a group and include all of the above plus participation in trips. The system for reprimands consists of three warnings for inappropriate behaviour after which a detention is given. A fourth warning means that the student is preventing learning and so is removed from the classroom, placed in the silent work room for the next two lessons and a letter sent home. There is a further level of meetings and exclusions if such behaviour continues during the term. A recent change to the structure of the school with the formation of four colleges with strong identities has introduced a degree of competitiveness between students to 'win' points for their college and so reinforces the system. Finally, the advice given in applying the policy is to be flexible; staff should try to have a one-to-one chat with a student before instigating official sanctions, using praise and rewards wherever possible, and using their instincts to modify the poor behaviour if appropriate.

The Emmbrook School Library

Whilst the library is obviously an important part of the school, it is also very different from a classroom and so, although I am aware of and can apply the 'managing behaviour for learning' policy, I tend to adapt it according to the circumstances. Classes coming into the library have to wait outside until either their teacher arrives for the lesson or I allow them to enter. This means that I can stand at the door and control the start of the lesson (whether it is one of my year 7 or year 8 library lessons or that of another year or subject), reminding them of the rules, reinforcing positive behaviour, praising them for entering quietly and sensibly, stopping them from moving chairs around and managing who sits where. I can also stop them picking up magazines, newspapers, the *Guinness Book of Records* and all the other wonderful distractions that we have as part of our libraries. It certainly is a paradox that the resources we buy in to attract users are the very ones that distract them when they should be working!

I see all Year 7 and Year 8 students for one hour every two weeks, so I am able to tell them the rules from the outset and they have no excuses for not knowing what they are. My main rule, and one that is easy to remember, is that students' behaviour should not disturb other library users… this means that I can apply slightly different parameters at breaks than I would during lessons. Off the main library I have the Sixth Form library (a quiet study area), the English Faculty office with seven members of staff and the College Leaders office with four members of staff, thus I am able to point out to students that at any time during the day there may be people working in those rooms that they should not disturb. It also helps to have staff around and indeed, several other teachers often use the library to work in – they tell me they like the space and the atmosphere – and I think this gives a very good message to students.

When it comes to managing behaviour, I think you have to be strict to begin with, consistent and mean what you say. It's no good telling a student that you'll move them if they carry on talking and then take no action. They will soon learn that their bad behaviour will not result in sanctions. When the students have got to know you and you have got to know them, you can relax a little. When I am talking to a class, I expect (like other members of staff) that students will be quiet and listen to me. If a student is talking, I will stop, tell them to be quiet and point out that talking whilst a member of staff is talking is rude and then carry on. I may also point out that they are preventing other students from learning and apologise to the rest of the class for the interruption. Sometimes, however, just a look or a shake of the head suffices. And if a student is fiddling with something or reading instead of listening then I may carry on talking but wander over to them and remove whatever it is that is distracting them, without breaking my stride or flow – it really does depend on the student.

I have to be honest and say that I do not strictly apply the warnings system. I will often only give one warning, tell them if they carry on I will move them and then do so – to another table with different students, to a table on their own (moving a table and chair into a corner if necessary), next to me or even put them outside on a chair thus removing them from their audience. Staff walking past invariably stop to ask what they have done plus it is often cold outside so they are usually keen to come back. I only leave them for a short time to give me a chance to settle the rest of the class and then speak to them before I allow them in again but this generally does the trick.

Sometimes I will just give one warning and tell the student in question that this is their first, second and third warning all in one because they have consistently misbehaved, I am fed up with their behaviour and I am too busy to be constantly interrupted by them. This will often bring a shocked response as they are used to three warnings but it does seem to work, possibly because they know I mean it! I write warnings in planners although this is usually for silly and inappropriate behaviour at breaktime rather than in lessons; I find teachers are more likely to follow the 'three warnings and writing in planners' structure than I am. As breaks are extremely busy, I cannot allow any sort of silliness that could result in accidents so I am quite immediate in my responses to such activities and will ban students if they continue. If I do this then I inform their tutor who will take the appropriate action – they obviously know whether this is another event in a series of misdemeanours or a one-off incident and whether a detention or a letter home is necessary. I have the full support of staff including the Head and senior management team in maintaining behaviour and discipline in the library which gives me confidence to deal with matters immediately, or to seek advice or escalation if necessary.

I do not give detentions very often myself but will readily give merits, commendations, bookmarks, etc. to students who I feel have worked and behaved exceptionally well. It is also surprising how smiley stickers are still popular with lower school students! At the end of the lesson I will praise the whole class if appropriate, pointing out what they did particularly well and, if they have had a reading lesson where they settled very quickly then I will reward them with 10 minutes of reading of their choice, which includes magazines and non-fiction books. Occasionally I will keep a whole class in for the first few minutes at break if they have taken too long to settle down and have been particularly disruptive. I then release students table by table, allowing the ones who were actually working quietly to go first, and I often find that the threat of this is enough to get them focused on what they are meant to be doing.

During research lessons, I walk around the room, making sure that students have found relevant information, that they are coping with the required information skills and that they do not need any further guidance or advice. This means that I can speak quietly to students not behaving appropriately and make sure they stay on task.

I find low level disruption is common in the school library; there are far too many distractions but such behaviour could be a sign that the class are getting bored... it does help to know the situation – is it a bottom set full of inveterate 'fiddlers' or a top set, can they follow what you are telling them or are they two steps ahead? Recognising this and adjusting your lesson can be useful and prevent further disruptions. However, if I have read a situation wrong and accused someone of misbehaving when it wasn't them (and believe me, the students will be the first to tell you if you have) then I will apologise. I don't make a big deal of it but I think it's important to acknowledge that you have made a mistake.

All of this, however, is easier if you know the students. As well as seeing them in library lessons throughout Years 7 and 8, I organise activities and clubs that bring me into contact with students and enable me, not only to learn their names but also to get to know them in a more relaxed setting.

Additionally, getting involved in other areas of school life, such as taking part in sports day, helping with charity events, going to see music and drama productions and accompanying trips can help you get to know them and your involvement in such activities will mean that they will see that you are part of the system, a member of the staff with the same level of authority.

Managing behaviour in the school library can be difficult. It is a different situation from the classroom, with students entering and leaving throughout the day, and this can be enough to cause disruption. Activities that occur there also vary. Whilst it is important to know what the overall school behavioural policy is, I think that librarians need to adapt this and be flexible in their approach.

Summary

- Don't take their behaviour or comments personally.
- Be strict to begin with and then relax.
- Carry through any sanctions or actions otherwise it won't be effective.

But... there will be times when you may have to just accept defeat. I had a Year 8 Set 4 English class, 12 boys in all, participating in a creative writing workshop with a visiting author. All was going well, they were producing some amazing stories and were then asked if they'd like to read their work aloud. One boy was exceedingly keen... 'the ball shot off his foot, straight into the goalkeeper... "arrggghhhhh, my penis, my penis, the goalkeeper yelled".' ... at that point I *knew* that there was no way I was ever going to keep the class quiet and stop those boys from rolling around the floor in fits of laughter!

Case Study 3: Bangor Grammar School

Ann Cowdrey

Librarian, Bangor Grammar School

Bangor Grammar School

Bangor Grammar School in Northern Ireland is a boys' 11–18 independent school of approx 900 students, including 200+ in the Sixth Form.

We are a voluntary grammar school with a rich history, having celebrated our sesquicentennial celebrations in 2006/2007. The library features in the School Development Plan and is also considered to be the 'heart of the school' (my Principal is an English teacher). This is demonstrated in the plans for our new school where it has been physically placed at the centre of the new building. All in all we don't have serious behaviour problems within the school as a whole. Discipline is consistent throughout the school, as the same standard of behaviour is expected from the pupils by both teaching and support staff, and for the most part the pupils treat all staff with respect and due deference. Everyone is singing from the same hymn sheet as it were.

'Behaviour Management' – perhaps this is the most dreaded topic for a school librarian. Straight away thoughts of horrendous lunch times spring to mind, a problem we all can surely identify with! On contemplation it struck me that behaviour management encompasses so much more than just those awful lunch times when the rain is pouring down outside a library jam-packed with jostling boys more intent on mayhem and mischief than well-mannered literary pursuits.

Being the 'new librarian' is daunting enough in any school but more so when your predecessor has been in the post for many years and there are long established traditions and rules in place. Initially I had to be seen as a force to be reckoned with, someone who said what they meant and meant what they said. At times this was tiring and I often felt as if things were never going to be any different and a career change started to look attractive! However, perseverance paid off and slowly but surely I began to establish myself with the pupils and the staff. I did intentionally set out to win over the hearts and minds of the junior school with the premise of 'Give me a child until he is seven and I will give you the man' in mind.

Perhaps the hardest group to deal with were those boys in the senior school. When I took up my post in Bangor Grammar School, almost five years ago, the library had become an area that Sixth Form felt was their exclusive domain. Their behaviour was challenging to say the least, in as much as they resented me and any new initiatives I introduced. It has taken, what could be considered a 'cycle', for that mindset to be broken down, but to be honest it has been well worth the struggle. Those now in the Sixth Form have really only known me as their librarian, having come up through the school adhering to my rules. Not only are these young men, on the whole, well mannered and showing evidence of having developed a work ethic not previously seen in former years, but they drop in for a 'chat' during lunch and break times. This may simply be a 'How's it going Miss?' to let me know about what is going on in their lives in general; or to look for a book or information. It's not by accident that I've mentioned the book and information last in the previous sentence as I have come to realise the importance of the pastoral care role in a school librarian's daily existence. What has this to do with behaviour management you may ask? It is, I believe, central to how the boys perceive the librarian. When junior pupils see a good relationship between senior students and the librarian it inevitably has a positive impact on their behaviour.

I work closely with the Sixth Form Study Supervisor to manage behaviour during study periods. Sixth Form may sign out of study to come to the library. Sometimes this is to work quietly at a table or else to use a computer. They have to sign into the library on a daily sign-in sheet which is collected at the end of the day by the Study Supervisor who then checks it against her list of boys who have signed out. This works well for us and the boys know that their attendance and behaviour both in study and the library is closely monitored. I have access to the RM Tutor programme on my computer, whereby I am able to keep a discreet eye on whether they are working or surfing. Those who don't comply with the acceptable use policy are told that there is only one warning. Should they persist in breaking the rules I send them back to study and mark the sign in sheet accordingly. The study supervisor will then withdraw library privileges for an appropriate period of time, according to the severity of the offence. Obviously if a pupil is a persistent offender then the time that they are withdrawn will be longer. The boys quickly come to realise that their use of the library is a privilege rather than a right. It is a simple system that works very effectively for our school, though I hasten to add that it has taken a few years to perfect.

In my opinion, one of the keys to managing behaviour, strange as it may seem, is to know the names of those pupils who use the library regularly. Not only does this personalise the service but it also serves as a deterrent to unruly behaviour. An identifiable pupil means that a name can easily be passed along to a Year Head or to a member of senior management. I only resort to this in the event of continual behaviour problems. I have full support from Senior Management and complete freedom to make decisions on library related matters. This has a knock on effect, as pupils know that they are not only accountable to me but to Senior Management if the need arises. It does take time to create a good working relationship and to let others know there is a point to what you do and that you are not simply a babysitter. I suppose what I am trying to say is that as with all children boundaries need to be set and this is no different in the library than it is within the home. Once the boundaries have been crossed I simply ask the pupil to leave and not return for the rest of that day and sometimes even longer. Having established myself as firm but fair I find that on many occasions a stern look is all that is necessary.

Wet weather is my greatest enemy. When I wake up to the sound of rain on the roof my heart sinks. I have therefore introduced 'wet weather passes' to control library usage on inclement days. I issue 60 of these passes and have found that although boys have one they do not always use it. I previously tried using lunch passes on a daily basis, but they don't work for me because they tended to make the library exclusive as opposed to inclusive. Not only did the use of these passes adversely affect borrowing statistics but it was only those boys who had been released from class first or were quickest at negotiating the corridors who managed to get them. The passes also caused problems in as much as they have been known to be 'sold' and even to cause fights, not to mention the numbers of boys clogging the corridor outside the library hoping to procure a pass by fair or foul means. But, in the absence of a better solution, the passes do help to keep the numbers of pupils in the library down to manageable proportions on wet days.

Numbers in the library are a problem to say the least. We are in the process of designing and building a new school and the concept of social areas has been flagged up as important, with such areas being included in the plans for the new school building. I feel that I have still to effectively solve the problem of keeping the library inclusive, whilst controlling the large numbers of boys who use it during both junior and senior lunch times. Sometimes the simplest measures are the most effective. I have found that chess sets are great for keeping young men occupied and indeed mine are used prolifically by both junior and senior pupils alike. In general I don't approve of groups of boys standing around, as this usually leads to horseplay. I have 26 computers, seating for a further 30 pupils at tables and for nine more in the soft seating areas. All of these seats are occupied before school, break time and lunch times. I have a prefect on duty in the library during the junior lunch period, as an extra pair of eyes is always useful. My junior librarians keep the issue desk manned enabling me to circulate, which is no doubt a deterrent to would-be miscreants. However, it seems to me to be a no win situation. By restricting numbers it limits the service the library can provide and I find that the facilities and resources are not necessarily being used by the right pupils for the right reason. Who are the right pupils and what is the right reason you may ask? I wish I had an answer for that. In my opinion the library should strive to create a level playing field, as it were, for all pupils. Not knowing the circumstances and needs of each pupil I feel it is wrong of me to judge or exclude a child simply because their idea of library use may not be the same as mine.

The pupils in Bangor Grammar School are by no means angels and junior lunch time is manic most days. Senior lunch tends to be quieter but only because Sixth Formers have a common room in which to socialise. To get to the point where behaviour is acceptable and manageable takes a lot of work and is indeed stressful. Perseverance, consistency and a good sense of humour are important and I have found that over time pupils come to know exactly how far they can push me before sanctions are put in place. Behaviour management takes up a lot of time but it is not a part of the job that can ever be ignored. In order to survive I had to really tough it out over the first few years in post so that I can now reap the benefits of good behaviour on a daily basis. I may still encounter some bad behaviour but since I have a firm set of rules in place and there is no doubt that potential offenders are aware of them, I can manage the miscreants without too much trouble. The hardest part is the time and effort that it takes to get to this point. Despite having to be constantly alert to behaviour issues, I love my job and wouldn't change it even for a school full of perfectly behaved children – if such a thing exists?

Case Study 4: Stromness Academy

Frances Sinclair

Librarian, Stomness Academy. SLYA Honour List 2005 and a member of the SLA Executive Committee 2005–2008

Stromness Academy

Stromness Academy is a 6 year (12–18yr olds) secondary school in the second largest town, Stromness, on the Orkney Islands, off the North coast of Scotland. The school roll currently stands at 434. Two thirds of pupils are bussed in from the catchment area of the West Mainland. Class sizes are small by most standards, being between 15 for practical groups and 24 pupils for register groups. Some certificate classes (S3 and above) can be as high as 30 pupils.

The Early Challenges

Arriving in a new job as a recent graduate is challenging at the best of times but taking up the role of a school librarian, whether as graduate or experienced librarian (from another sector) can be a baptism of fire. Not only do you have a library to run but you have to deal with a wide range of young people accompanied by all their social, emotional and behavioural issues.

As a graduate arriving in my post at Stromness Academy in 1992 I didn't know what I was letting myself in for. The post had been vacant for at least six months, the library was a mess and although there was a 'code of conduct' in place the pupils generally did as they pleased. I came in fairly confident I could deal with anything but I didn't count on the teenager: their perceived independence, 'I know better than you' attitude, and their capacity for disregarding the rules in place.

The school did have a discipline procedure in place but at that time, all I could really do was 'ask' pupils to leave the library if their behaviour was unacceptable and report it to my line manager (then the Head Teacher) or another member of SMT. It did get to the stage that certain pupils just came into the library (at lunchtime) to get a reaction out of me, which in the early days they did, and I am sure it was a game to see how many times they could get chucked out. At that time lines or detention was only meted out by the teaching staff so I felt that I had no authority to deal with discipline issues and the pupils knew it. Swearing (at staff i.e. me) or fighting was reported to SMT and pupils were banned from the library for a short period or in some cases actually excluded from school.

Most of the behavioural problems were of a low level nature – lack of respect, misusing resources, too much chatting and noise and more often than not I could send them out of the library. If a pupil refused to do what I asked, then my stubborn streak kicked in and I just continued to firmly request that they leave the library. In those days the voice was raised more often than I care to remember and once you shout the pupils have won!

Until the school had a review of behaviour policy my only recourse for any misdemeanour was to send the pupils out of the library. I hadn't heard of positive behaviour or a behaviour hierarchy at that point.

Use of the Library and discipline issues

It quickly became obvious that there were two distinct types of use of the library: class time and 'leisure' time (lunchtime) and each had their distinct problems.

Class Time

There were few discipline issues when a whole class (at that time class sizes were around 27 pupils) came to the library accompanied by their teacher. In this case the teacher had responsibility for the pupils yet I often took the lead in maintaining good discipline as I suppose the staff didn't want to 'tread on my toes'. Problems occurred when pupils were sent either as individuals or groups of up to half a class. This meant that at times there could be 15 – 20 or more pupils in the library with no teacher present and these pupils often used a visit to the library as a skive. Combined with S6 (Y12) using the Upper Library for study (hah!), an awkward library layout meant that supervision of all parts of the library was particularly difficult especially due to the fact my workspace consisted of a desk squeezed into a 2m^2 'cupboard' with no view of the library. The redesign of the issue desk to include a workspace for me, meant I had a suitable vantage point from which I could see some of the library.

One of the earliest policies drawn up in liaison with the Library Committee to help with behaviour management, still (mostly) effectively used today was 'Class Time Use of the Library'. It states the number of pupils who may be sent, and who (teacher and/or librarian) is responsible for the pupils. More often than not there is a member of the Support for Learning staff present in the library which means another adult is available if needed.

CLASS TIME USE OF LIBRARY

INDIVIDUALS / SMALL GROUPS [5 pupils]: [Ad hoc basis]
Pupils may be sent to the library to select books, use reference material, use the computers or do written work. A teacher may send up to 5 pupils for this purpose without prior consultation with the Librarian.

On arrival pupils should report to the Librarian indicating the teacher they came from and what they intend to do. The conduct of pupils present in the library on this basis is the responsibility of the Librarian whose response to misconduct should be to send the pupil(s) back to the classroom. If the library is very busy the Librarian may have to send pupils back to class.

LARGER GROUPS [6 or more pupils]: Staff intending to send more than 5 pupils during class-time should **consult with the Librarian in advance**. The Librarian and the class-teacher will be responsible for the conduct of these pupils. The teacher should be present for some, but not necessarily all, of the time. **Pupils should report to the Librarian on arrival in the library.**

CLASSES: Whole class use <u>**must**</u> be arranged with the Librarian in advance. Staff must be present for all of the time. Any teacher from any department can timetable a regular slot for class work, particularly, for example, for short-term projects that require library-based research.

N.B. Access may be restricted when the Librarian is teaching Library and Information Skills. You will be informed via the bulletin when this happens.

If you don't intend to bring booked groups or your class to the library please let Mrs Sinclair know as soon as possible.

There are still issues with low-level incidents during class time and one of the most wearing aspects is disciplining other teacher's classes when they are ignoring them or doing their marking or speaking to individual pupils about their work. It is possible teachers feel they are treading on my toes when they are in 'my department' but such discipline matters is a joint matter. Staff are reminded of the above policy on regular occasions.

Pupils' free time/Non-Curriculum Time
Non-curriculum time can bring its own problems as pupils want to relax and enjoy themselves, not necessarily in a manner appropriate in the library situation. Not only that, there are pupils of different ages and abilities that need to be catered for and the library is used for different purposes. At Stromness, non-curriculum time includes before registration, lunchtimes and after school as well as S6 pupils on so called 'free' periods when they have time out of class.

Before registration and after school
Pupils bussed in from our catchment area can start arriving as early as 8:15am. The library officially opens at 8:40 but more often than not I open it as I get into work at 8:30 when the Pupil Librarians come in to help.

The library is also available after school until 4pm but few folk take it up due to needing to get the bus home, except on Tuesdays when after school activities take place both in the library and elsewhere in the school.

In the time I have been in the school, there have been no discipline problems at these times.

S6 'Free' periods

Most S6 pupils are not on a full timetable therefore they have free periods during which they are encouraged to use the library for study. A separate study area is available for them in the Upper Library and it is designated a silent area. A 'Code of Conduct' was in place when I arrived in post and this has since been up-dated to be more positively phrased (mostly).

Use of Upper Library

1. Use the Upper library for individual private study.

2. Sign in and out on the form on the issue desk indicating time of arrival and time of leaving.

3. Work in SILENCE.
   [During Lunchtime the rule of silence will be relaxed slightly in keeping with the atmosphere in the Lower Library. Pupils may discuss their work quietly.]

4. Pupils looking at the Careers Section during class time should do so quietly, preferably in silence!

5. No food or drink should be taken into or consumed in the library.

6. Personal stereos/MP3 players may be used but should be turned down to avoid disturbing others.

7. Switch off mobile phones.

   If the Upper Library is not being used appropriately then pupils may be asked to leave and/or the Upper Library will be closed.

Most of the discipline issues with S6 and their use of the library generally involve them making too much noise and ignoring my instructions. Although in itself it is minor, this can be one of the most stressful things to deal with as giving constant reminders proves wearing. All S6 are informed of their responsibilities during registration, the induction conference and through reminders on the daily bulletin. In the past I have given too many warnings, in the hope that the message gets through but more recently I have used the discipline hierarchy, giving them a warning, then the choice to leave, and then finally telling pupils to leave. I liaise closely with the head of year in this matter.

LUNCHTIME USE OF LIBRARY

WHY ARE YOU COMING TO THE LIBRARY AT LUNCHTIME?
To do homework?
Use the computers?
Study?
Do some research?
Read books?
Read magazines?
Use CD Rom?
Use the Internet?

IF YES TO ANY OF THESE THEN YOU MAY COME IN!

Don't bother if you are going to:
Just stand around or wander about
Chat noisily
Disturb other pupils or staff.

Lunchtime

Most use of the library is at lunchtime and this can be a flashpoint because the diversity of pupils who come into the library. We have a core of 20 to 25 pupils who use the library every day and in general they behave themselves very well, if not a little noisily at times. They keep themselves occupied using the computers for games, playing 'Magic the Gathering', creating 'Dungeon and Dragons' characters and adventures or just 'chilling out' in the reading zone on the couch and beanbags.

It is hard to get away from the fact that the library is used as a 'refuge' by a number pupils, particularly pupils who aren't in with the 'in crowd', those with Aspergers and similar conditions, and those who don't like the noise and chaotic atmosphere in the social areas. The library users have been labelled, and there are certain elements in the school who do like to see if they can get a rise out of them. Thankfully my regulars are mature and intelligent enough to ignore them. A handful of these pupils have been known to be rather volatile and although generally well behaved it only takes someone goading or upsetting them to cause an incident such as a fight.

As the school has a split lunch it means that classes might be in at the same time as those on lunch break. A teacher (usually) is always present with a whole class so I can often focus on supervising the lunchtime users who in the main understand they need to be quiet and keep out of the way.

When I started at the school the library was meant to be used for research and study purposes only at lunchtime. Trying to get 20 plus pupils to knuckle down and work during their free time proved to be futile. By the late 1990s lunchtime rules had been relaxed to allow for leisure use of computers (games) and leisure reading but I still insisted on everyone being occupied. The computers still had work priority and the pupils playing games quickly learnt to give up their booking to pupils requiring to work. By this time I had become more confident in handling the pupils but still didn't have the procedures to deal with indiscipline. By the early 2000s the rules were relaxed further… pupils could now come in to sit and chat quietly. Also role-playing games were introduced by pupils themselves and meant productive activity being carried out.

At lunchtime, I am usually on my own with 20 – 30+ pupils. SMT do try to pop in from time to time but duties elsewhere often mean the library doesn't receive a visit.

Low level behavioural issues that arise regularly at lunchtime include:

- Noise levels
- Minor bickering
- Pupils just standing or wandering around.
- Physical 'play' – boisterous
- Too many pupils at computers

Action taken: reminders and warnings in line with the discipline hierarchy, referral to SMT for non-compliance.

Serious incidents (rare but stressful at the time):

- Fighting
- Swearing at staff
- Bullying
- Refusing to follow instructions.

Action Taken: Referral to SMT.

In the case of a fight I do not attempt to physically stop it but use proximity and a firm loud voice to try and calm the situation, having also asked another pupil to go and find help from SMT. Thankfully I am usually able to intervene before fists start flying. It does mean I have to be very observant.

Fights are rare but it became clear that I would send a pupil to find SMT only to have them come back to say they couldn't. Thankfully in most cases the fight had stopped and I had managed to keep at least one of the protagonists in the library. This meant I needed to ensure there was a policy in place.

Procedures during a fight:

- Proximity.
- Tell another pupil to fetch help from SMT. Pupil Librarians are shown how to phone the lower office.
- Repetition! Firm voice, deep tones. I usually target one pupil and repeat 'back-off' using their name often.
- Separate protagonists, keep at least one in the library who is told firmly to sit at a table until SMT arrive.
- SMT to deal with follow-up.

New Behaviour Management Procedures

Whole School

About 8–10 years ago the school reviewed its behaviour management procedures and provided the whole staff with training opportunities for 'Assertive Discipline' and 'Positive Behaviour' in which I took part. Conduct cards were brought in for S1 and S2 and for the first time I was able to be involved in discipline procedures, being allowed to mark conduct cards or give detentions. I have never had the need to do so as the system of warnings appears to do its job. I was involved in the various working parties and a key player in policy making, in particular relating to the mobile phone and personal music player policy.

Pupils are informed of the behaviour expectations through posters, verbal reinforcement and the school and library codes of conduct are in the pupil planners, along with the new (2008) trial merit system and a revised version of the conduct cards. Recognising good behaviour (Celebrating Success) has become a priority this session.

Sanctions for inappropriate behaviour from whole school policy that I could employ in the library:

- Verbal reminder
- Change of seat
- Mark conduct card (S1/2) (Only useful for use in class time as pupils tend not to carry planners with them during their free time)
- Detention
- Referral to class teacher/SMT.

Behaviour Expectations in the Library

As a result of the work done in school and at School Library Association in Scotland national branch training events, I revised my library code of conduct.

Code of Conduct

1. Visit the library to read, use resources, study, do research or use computers. If coming from class. Enter the library in an orderly manner.

2. Behave calmly and quietly and be considerate of other users (staff or pupils).

3. No food or drink.

4. Switch off mobile phones and personal music players.

5. Get all resources issued by the Librarian.

6. Leave the library neat and tidy.

S1 pupils have been taught behaviour expectations in the library before they make their first visit for Library induction for three years now. They are first reminded of the school code within the context of the library:

Behaviour Expectations in the Library

The School Code of Conduct applies in the Library with particular reference to the following:

- Follow instructions

- Listen without interrupting

- Speak quietly and politely

- Tidy up before you leave

- Display good behaviour at all times

They are then shown a PowerPoint presentation during which they are asked to consider:

- Why do you think there are rules in the library?
- What rules do you think there should be?
- Why do you have to look after books?
- How can you help to avoid damaging books?
- What do you think is acceptable use of the library – during class/during free time?

Extracts from S1 Library Induction Week One presentation

What do you think is acceptable use of the library?

Homework   Info Skills

Choose & read   Internet for
books   research

Find info for
a project

Word
processing

CD Rom

All quietly without too much chatter!

BUT WHAT ABOUT YOUR FREE TIME?

Free Time in the Library

Before Registration

Lunchtime

After School

Homework   Study   Research
Use computers – Internet / CD Rom / Word Processing
Read

Sit and chat quietly
Play games on computer
Play chess or other games

```
┌─────────────────────────────────────────────────────┐
│  ┌───────────────────────────────────────────────┐  │
│  │   What happens if you don't behave properly?  │  │
│  └───────────────────────────────────────────────┘  │
│  CLASS TIME                                          │
│                                                      │
│   1.   Verbal warning                                │
│   2.   Reminder with choice to move to another seat  │
│   3.   Move with possibility of returning to original seat │
│   4.   Return to classroom.                          │
│        Your conduct card in your Student Planner may be │
│                       marked.                        │
│                                                      │
│  FREE TIME (Before registration, Lunch, After School)│
│                                                      │
│   1.   Verbal warning                                │
│   2.   Reminder with choice to move seats or leave library │
│   3.   Move or leave library with possibility of returning │
│   4.   Leave library                                 │
│                                                      │
└─────────────────────────────────────────────────────┘
```

This procedure means I can make it clear to pupils what is expected of them during their time using the library. I believe that formally discussing your expectations with them lets them know you mean business and the guidelines are clear.

Discipline Hierarchy during Class Time

Individuals or small groups

1. Reminder
2. Reminder with choice to move
3. Move with possibility of returning
4. Return to class
5. Severe clause: referral to teacher or SMT

Whole classes [cooperation with teacher]

1. Reminder
2. Reminder with choice to move
3. Move with possibility of returning
4. Take out behaviour card [S1/2] / Dealt with by Teacher [S3-6]
5. Mark behaviour card [S1/2]
6. Usually returned to classroom to work on own!!!
7. Severe clause – teacher's responsibility

Discipline Hierarchy during Free Time

1. Reminder
2. Reminder with choice to move or leave library
3. Move or leave library with possibility of returning
4. Leave library
5. Severe clause – refer to SMT – Banned

How 'new approaches' have affected behaviour management in the library

My attitude has developed.

- I now use a more positive approach. I shout less and use praise and rewards more frequently. We all know this is more effective, but old habits can die hard.

- I am more conscious of using my voice – calmly and firmly.

- I try to choose my words carefully, trying not to be too hasty in my reactions.

- I try to reduce stress in a situation. Keeping calm and breathing slowly will help.

Has pupil behaviour improved or am I just better at management and calmer about it? I think it is a bit of both. Experience and self-confidence both count in the long run, but above all – get to know your pupils, operate within school policies, be approachable and love your job.

Check List

Your present status/working conditions

Please ✓ or ✗ as appropria[te]

Seen as an equal with teaching staff – rights/responsibilities	
Have a clear and adequate line management structure	
Have regular contact with your line manager	
Have a clear job description	
Join appropriate meetings	
Regularly visit the staff room to chat with colleagues	
Are a part of the school's appraisal scheme	
Have knowledge about school developments	
Have knowledge and understanding of school policies	
Have appropriate curriculum knowledge	
Understand your current literacy development role	
Appear in the staff handbook	
Have been part of the inspection process	
Lead appropriate staff training sessions	
Join appropriate staff training sessions	
Take part in new induction sessions – staff, parents etc	
Take part in parents' evenings	
Have regular access to professional development	
Have regular time for meal breaks away from the LRC	
Have the support of other staff	

What have we missed?

Check List: Perceptions

What is the LRC for?   Who thinks what?

What happens if the groups have different perceptions?

s it a place to: T for teaching staff, **S** for students, **L** for LRC staff, **SMT** for Senior Management Team

keep dry and warm	
read the TES and look for another job	
browse the shelves and ICT	
do some homework/unfinished work using ICT or books	
do some revision – for a test/exam/SATs/GCSE etc	
use if PE/Games is impossible	
raise literacy standards and student performance	
find out what's on TV tonight or talk about last night's TV	
find some project/coursework information	
use as an exam room and maybe use LRC staff to invigilate	
hold a meeting	
eat lunch/have a drink	
chat with friends	
enjoy a good read	
casually read a paper or magazine	
send/receive emails/text messages/phonecalls/ring tones etc	
send disruptive students	
talk to library staff about problems at home	
practise information literacy/learning to learn skills	
enjoy a sweet/chewing gum	
do a detention	
learn more about a hobby/interest	
copy/print off somebody else's homework	
play a computer game	
have a game of chess or similar	
put a sick student	
mark a pile of assignments	
put a class in the absence of a teacher	
use a photocopier or scanner	
listen to a personal stereo	

Check List:
Rewards and Sanctions

Do they support your behaviour management style and positive LRC use?

What reward system do you use for good behaviour?
In what ways does it match or differ from the general school policy?
What sanctions do you use? – and are they effective?
In what ways do these match the general school policies?

Articles

There are many articles in the educational press – in particular the *Times Educational Supplement* on behaviour and related issues in school – keep a look out for them, clip and file them in your LRC staff development section and notify colleagues with a behaviour responsibility.

Books

There are many excellent books about the subject of behaviour, working with young people in education, understanding body language and stress relief. Those with any schools focus tend to be written from the teacher/classroom viewpoint.

Those that we recommend include:

BREALEY, Erica. *Ten Minute Stress Relief*. Chancellor Press, 2003. 978-0-7537-0736-4

BIGGS, Victoria. *Caged in Chaos: A Dyspraxic Guide to Breaking Free*. Jessica Kingsley Publishers, 2005. 978-1-84310-347-9

COWLEY, Sue. *Getting the Buggers to Behave*. Third Edition, Continuum, 2006. 978-0-8264-8912-8

DUNN, Roger. *Do's and Don'ts of Behaviour Management: A Teacher's Survival Guide*. Continuum, 2005. 978-0-8264-8464-2

GORDON, Gerard. *Managing Challenging Children*. Prim-Ed Publishing, 1996. 978-1-86400-302-4

GRAY, John. *Men are from Mars, Women are from Venus, Children are from Heaven: How to Have Strong, Confident Children*. Continuum, 1999. 978-0-09-182616-1

GRIFFITHS, Alex and STEPHENSON, Pauline. *101 Essential Lists On Managing Behaviour in the Secondary School*. Continuum 2006. 978-0-8264-8864-0

HOOK, Peter and VASS, Andy. *Behaviour Management Pocketbook*. Teachers' Pocketbooks, 2004. 978-1-903776-59-9

HOWARTH, Roy. *100 Ideas for Supporting Pupils with Social, Emotional and Behavioural Difficulties*. Continuum, 2008. 978-0-8264-9661-4

JONES, Josh [aged 11]. *Do You Know About ADHD Sir?* ADDISS, 2006. 978-0-9554033-1-6

LAMBERT, David and The Diagram Group. *Body Language: How to Understand the Unspoken Language of the Body*. Collins Gem, 2004. 978-0-00-718992-2

LINDENFIELD, Gael. *Confident Teens: How to Raise a Positive, Confident and Happy Teenager*. Thorsons, 2001. 978-0-00-710062-0

Further Reading

PEASE, Allan and Barbara. *The Definitive Book of Body Language: How to Read Others' Attitudes by Their Gestures*. Orion, 2005. 978-0-75285-878-4

QUILLIAM, Susan. *Body Language: Make the Most of Your Professional and Personal Life by Learning to Read and Use the Body's Secret Signals*. Carlton Books, 2004. 978-1-84442-675-1

RAYMENT, Tabatha. *Managing Boys' Behaviour*. Continuum, 2006. 978-0-8264-8501-4

RELF, Peter, HIRST, Rod, RICHARDSON, Jan and YOUDELL, Georgina. *Best Behaviour: Starting Points for Effective Behaviour Management*. Network Educational Press Ltd, 1998. 978-1-85539-046-1

ROGERS, Bill. *Behaviour Management: A Whole School Approach*. Paul Chapman Publishing, 2000. 978-0-7619-6929-7

ROGERS, Bill. *Classroom Behaviour: A Practical Guide to Effective Teaching, Behaviour Management and Colleague Support*. Paul Chapman Publishing, 2002. 978-0-7619-4018-0

ROGERS, Bill. *Cracking the Hard Class: Strategies for Managing the Harder Than Average Class*. Paul Chapman Publishing, 2000. 978-0-7619-6928-0

ROGERS, Bill ed. *How To Manage Children's Challenging Behaviour*. Paul Chapman Publishing, 2004. 978-1-4129-0217-5

ROBERTSON, John. *Effective Classroom Control*. Hodder & Stoughton, 2000. 978-0-340-64814-8

SEVERE, Sal. *How to Behave So Your Children Will, Too!* Vermillion, 2004. 978-0-09-188764-3

STALLARD, Paul. *Think Good – Feel Good: A Cognitive Behaviour Therapy Workbook for Children and Young People*. Wiley, 2002. 978-0-470-84290-4

YOUNG, Johnnie. *100+ Ideas for Managing Behaviour*. Continuum, 2007. 978-0-8264-9316-3

We also recommend three books on teenage brain development that helps explain behaviour:

MORGAN, Nicola. *Blame My Brain: The Amazing Teenage Brain Revealed*. Walker Books, 2005. 978-1-4063-1116-7

MORGAN, Nicola. *Know Your Brain: Feed It, Test It, Stretch It*. Walker Books, 2007. 978-1-4063-0415-2

STRAUCH, Barbara. *Why Are They So Weird? What's Really Going on inside a Teenager's Brain*. Bloomsbury, 2003, rev 2004. 978-0-7475-6848-3

Reports

ADHD WORKING GROUP. *Attention Deficit Hyperactivity Disorder (ADHD): A Practical Guide for Schools.* 2004.
http://www.education-support.org.uk/parents/special-education/adhd/

DEPARTMENT OF EDUCATION AND SCIENCE (Republic of Ireland). *School Matters: The Report of the Task Force on Student Behaviour in Second Level Schools.* 2006.
http://www.education.ie/servlet/blobservlet/tfsb_index.htm

ESTYN. *Behaviour in Wales: Good Practice in Managing Challenging Behaviour.* Ref.G/636/05-06. 2006. 978-0-7504-4019-6
http://www.estyn.gov.uk/publications/Behaviour_in_Wales.pdf

HMIE (Scotland). *Case Studies of Good Practice in Improving the Climate for Learning.* 2006. http://www.hmie.gov.uk/documents/publication/hmie_csgp.html

NATIONAL AUTISTIC SOCIETY. Report for Autism Awareness Week 2002. *Autism in Schools: Crisis or Challenge.* 2002. 978-1-899280-71-1
http://www.autism.org.uk

NATIONAL FOUNDATION FOR EDUCATIONAL RESEARCH. (Anne Wilkin; Helen Moor; Jenny Murfield; Kay Kinder and Fiona Johnson) *Behaviour in Scottish Schools.* Scottish Executive, 2006. 0-7559-6266-4
http://www.scotland.gov.uk/Publications/2006/09/28125634/0

OFSTED. *Managing Challenging Behaviour.* Doc. Ref. HMI 2363. 2005
http://www.ofsted.gov.uk/Ofsted-home/Publications-and-research/Browse-all-by/Care/Childcare/Managing-challenging-behaviour

OFSTED. *Improving Behaviour: Lessons Learned From HMI Monitoring of Secondary Schools Where Behaviour Had Been Judged Unsatisfactory.* 2006.
http://www.ofsted.gov.uk/content/download/1873/12482/file/Improving%20behaviour%20(PDF%20format).pdf

STEER, Sir Alan (Chair). *Learning Behaviour: The Report of the Practitioners' Group on School Behaviour and Discipline.* DfES, 2005. Ref. DfES-1950-20005DOC-EN 2005. 978-1-84478-599-5
http://www.dcsf.gov.uk/behaviourandattendance/about/learning_behaviour.cfm

Further Reading

Websites

DCSF resources:

There are many useful resources about Behaviour and Attendance listed under the National Strategies Key Stage 3 website, see

http://www.standards.dfes.gov.uk/secondary/keystage3/all/respub/ba_km

and

http://www.standards.dfes.gov.uk/secondary/keystage3/respub/behaviour

http://inclusion.ngfl.gov.uk/index.php?l=253&incWebsiteTopicid=19

> Websites listed on the theme of Challenging behaviour, challenging inclusion.

Other resources:

http://www.betterbehaviourscotland.gov.uk/

> Know Better Behaviour (Scottish Executive).

http://www.behaviour4learning.ac.uk/

> Behaviour4Learning.

http://www.atl.org.uk/help-and-advice/classroom- behaviour/managing-behaviour.asp

> Guidance to schools from the Association of Teachers and Lecturers on the legal side of behaviour management – well worth a look.

http://www.autism.org.uk/nas/jsp/polopoly.jsp?d=1071&a=8385

> The National Autistic Society – behaviour guidelines (for those with autism spectrum disorder).

http://www.behaviour4learning.ac.uk

> The site provides access to the research and evidence base informing teacher education.

http://www.educational-psychologist.co.uk/adhdclassrm.htm

> Managing Attention Deficit Disorder in the classroom.

http://www.healthyschools.gov.uk

> Useful for linking good health, behaviour and achievement.

http://www.ich.ucl.ac.uk/gosh_families/information_sheets/behaviour_problems_autism_families

> Joint website of Great Ormond Street Hospital for Children NHS Trust (GOSH) and UCL Institute of Child Health (ICH) – this website offers guidelines on ways to manage children with autism.

http://www.nasen.org.uk

> An excellent website for those interested in Special Educational Needs education.

http://www.nelig.com

> The website of the National Emotional Literacy Interest Group.

http://www.netdoctor.co.uk/diseases/facts/adhd.htm
Net Doctor, for some clear information about ADHD.

http://www.teachernet.gov.uk/wholeschoolbehaviour
Teachernet lists other useful government websites about behaviour management.

Videos

Do have a look at the material on Teachers TV for further useful ideas:
http://www.teachers.tv/behaviour

Student Monitoring Software

AB Tutor Control
http://www.abconsulting.com/html/Tutor_Control.html

Impero Software
http://www.imperosoftware.com

Net Support School
http://www.netsupportschool.com/index.asp

SynchronEyes Classroom Management
http://downloads.zdnet.co.uk/0,1000000375,39386627s,00.htm

Real VNC
http://www.realvnc.com

Other publications from the SLA

Paperwork Made Easy: Policy Making and Development Planning for the Secondary School Library

by Lynn Winkworth and Geoff Dubber

Putting together and then regularly updating a policy and a development plan is part of the essential work of everyone who runs an effective secondary school library. This updated and revised Guideline Plus gives you all the basics you need to do both jobs. It takes you carefully through the steps needed to produce a realistic and comprehensive policy and again gives you the route to produce a credible and meaningful development plan.

The core text of the previous edition has been revised and the authors have included a range of new policies, new opening statements to policies and new development plans. A supplementary volume containing further examples of policies and developments is available exclusively to SLA members on our website: http://www.sla.org.uk/paperwork/

£12.00 (to SLA members £9.00)

ISBN: 978-1-903446-47-8 (revised edition 2008)

Blogs and Bytes: ICT and the Secondary School Library

by Marianne Bradnock

ICT is assuming an increasingly important role in the work of the school librarian, totally changing our working lives in the last decade. It is essential then that the place of the library in a school's ICT strategy is well defined and that the librarian has the vision and knowledge to maintain a high profile in this rapidly developing area of work.

This comprehensive new guideline will provide detailed information and inspiration to practitioners new and experienced, covering issues such as supporting professional practice, using ICT to find information, supporting learners, ICT for reader development, Health & Safety issues and ICT and the law.

£12.00 (to SLA members £9.00)

ISBN: 978-1-903446-41-6 (published June 2007)

School Library Association